TALK BOURBON TO ME!

A whiskey lover's guide to
Kentucky's favorite spirit

Kim — Thanks for giving me permission
to use your Rockin' Whiskey Sour image!
It's a perfect fit for the book. Enjoy!

BETH UNDERWOOD

Best Regards —

A Toast

To Bourbon—To those who produce it,
those who consume it, and all who keep the tradition of
America's Native Spirit alive and well.

Front cover image credit: Drew Fritz, drewfritz.com
Back cover image by the author

© Copyright 2016
Beth Underwood, 26 Letter Press
ISBN-13: 978-1540509253
ISBN-10: 1540509257

INTRODUCTION

I first ran across *The Practical Distiller* while exploring the millions of books available in the public domain. As most residents of the Bluegrass state can attest, when one finds anything that hints of bourbon, whiskey, distilling or brewing—and because we all know there are unwritten rules on behaving as a good Kentuckian—such a find requires examination.

Honestly, I knew very little about bourbon before taking on this project, and will be the first to admit that's a crying shame for someone claiming to be a native Kentuckian. Lest I lose my Kentucky Colonel status, I decided it was time to become an expert—or at least learn enough to carry on an intelligent conversation with friends.

All things considered, the art and science of distilling hasn't changed much. Written more than 200 years ago, *The Practical Distiller* contains almost everything one would need to know about the process. The distilling culture, on the other hand, has grown exponentially. So I figured why not blend the time-honored tradition of distilling with a crash course of sorts on everything bourbon.

To that end, I visited several local distilleries, whose owners, operators and employees were as gracious as all get out. (That's *extremely* gracious in Kentucky-speak.) I came to know some of the industry pundits via social media—true aficionados on everything whiskey. I tried more than a few bourbons along the way, as well, which included a Sunday afternoon distillery tour with my dad and son that highlighted said adventures. (What better way to share good bourbon than with family?)

The pages that follow give you a look at what I discovered, and the phenomenon that is Kentucky Bourbon. It's found in some of the most decadent desserts and in the Kentucky Derby's favorite drink. It's been the subject of conversation—and controversy—on Capitol Hill and Hollywood. There are rules for tasting it and dates for celebrating it. Moreover, Kentucky's favorite whiskey opens the doors to a new world that reaches far beyond the borders of the Commonwealth. It's a community grounded in rich tradition and enduring excellence that invites everyone to join in. One could spend a lifetime learning about bourbon, and many do. My hope is that *Talk Bourbon to Me* will entice you to start your own explorations.

Beth Underwood
Lexington, Kentucky
November 2016

—

This project includes the entire manuscript of the 1809 book titled:

THE PRACTICAL DISTILLER
OR

AN INTRODUCTION TO MAKING WHISKEY, GIN, BRANDY, AND SPIRITS OF BETTER QUALITY, AND IN LARGER QUANTITIES, THAN PRODUCED BY THE PRESENT MODE OF DISTILLING, FROM THE PRODUCE OF THE UNITED STATES: SUCH AS RYE, CORN, BUCK-WHEAT, APPLES, PEACHES, POTATOES, PUMPIONS AND TURNIPS. WITH DIRECTIONS HOW TO CONDUCT AND IMPROVE THE PRACTICAL PART OF DISTILLING IN ALL ITS BRANCHES. TOGETHER WITH DIRECTIONS FOR PURIFYING, CLEARING, COLORING WHISKEY, MAKING SPIRITS SIMILAR TO FRENCH BRANDY, etc., FROM THE SPIRITS OF RYE, CORN, APPLES, POTATOES, etc, AND SUNDRY EXTRACTS OF APPROVED RECEIPTS FOR MAKING CIDER, DOMESTIC WINES, AND BEER.

BY SAMUEL McHARRY
OF LANCASTER COUNTY, PENN.
—1809—

Talk Bourbon to Me

TABLE OF CONTENTS

A sketch from inside Glenns Creek Distillery, which operates on the site of the former Old Crowe Distillery.

Chapter 1

OBSERVATIONS ON YEAST

That yeast is the main spring in distilling, is acknowledged by all distillers, though but few of them understand it, either in its nature or operation; though many pretend a knowledge of the grand subject of fermentation, and affect to understand the best mode of making stock yeast, and to know a secret mode unknown to all others—when it is my belief they know very little about it; but, by holding out the idea of adding some drug, not to be procured at every house, which has a hard name, and that is little known to people of common capacities: Such as Dragons blood, etc.. frequently retailing their secret, as the best possible mode of making stock yeast, at ten, twenty, and in some instances one hundred dollars. Confessing it a subject, abstruse, and a science little understood in Pennsylvania, and notwithstanding the numerous experiments I have made with care and close observation, yet from a consciousness of not understanding it, *too well*, I have in several instances purchased receipts, and made faithful experiments; but have never yet met the man of science, theory, or practice, whose mode of making stock yeast, yielded

a better preparation for promoting fermentation, than the simple mode pursued by myself for some years, and which I have uniformly found to be the best and most productive.

In making yeast, all drugs and witchcraft are unnecessary—Cleanliness, in preserving the vessels perfectly sweet, good malt, and hops, and an industrious distiller, capable of observation, and attention to the following receipt, which will be assuredly found to contain the essence and spirit of the ways and art of making that composition, a knowledge of which I have acquired, by purchases—consultations with the most eminent brewers, bakers, and distillers in this commonwealth, and above all, from a long practice and experience, proving its utility and superior merits to my most perfect satisfaction; and which I with pleasure offer to my fellow-citizens, as meriting a preference— notwithstanding the proud and scientific chemist, and the flowery declarations or treatises of the profound theorist, may

So this is where it all began. Well, sort of. By the time this book was written in 1808, more than a few settlers were experimenting in the art and science of distilling spirits. But we're still a few years away from the use of the term bourbon, so this is as good a time as any to dispense a hard and fast rule: All bourbon is whiskey. But not all whiskey is bourbon!

Prompted by his farm manager at his home in Mount Vernon, founding father George Washington entered the distilling business in 1797, with two stills that produced 600 gallons of whiskey. That winter, he approved the distillery's expansion, and by 1799, his distillery produced 11,000 gallons and was the largest in the nation.

One more thing. Rumor has it the whiskey cake was one of his favorites. Luckily for us all, the recipe for that cake just happens to be featured at the end of Chapter 3.

disapprove this simple mode, and offer those which they presume to be better, though they never soiled a finger in making a practical experiment, or perhaps witnessed a process of any description.

RECEIPT FOR STOCK YEAST: FOR A STOCK YEAST VESSEL OF TWO GALLONS, THE SIZE BEST ADAPTED FOR THAT PURPOSE

Take one gallon good barley malt, (be sure it be of good quality) put it into a clean, well scalded vessel, (which take care shall be perfectly sweet) pour thereon four gallons scalding water, (be careful your water be clean) stir the malt and water with a well scalded stick, until thoroughly mixed together, then cover the vessel close with a clean cloth, for half an hour; then uncover it and set it in some convenient place to settle, after three or four hours, or when you are sure the sediment of the malt is settled to the bottom, then pour off the top, or thin part that remains on the top, into a clean well scoured iron pot, (be careful not to disturb the thick sediment

Most historians agree that by the time Louisville, Kentucky, was founded in the late 1700s, the area's earliest inhabitants were already distilling. Known for its limestone-rich streams and springs, distillers were drawn to Frankfort, Owensboro and Bardstown. Today, Bardstown has the high honor of "Bourbon Capital of the World".

in the bottom, and that none of it goes into the pot); then add four ounces good hops, and cover the pot close with a clean scalded iron cover, and set it on a hot fire of coals to boil—boil it down one third, or rather more, then strain all that is in the pot through a thin hair sieve, (that is perfectly clean) into a clean well scalded earthen crock that is glazed—then stir into it, with a clean stirring stick, as much superfine flour as will make it about half thick, that is neither thick nor thin, but between the two, stirring it effectually until there be no lumps left in it. If lumps are left, you will readily perceive that the heart or inside of those lumps will not be scalded, and of course, when the yeast begins to work, those lumps will sour very soon, and of course sour the yeast—stir it then until those lumps are all broken, and mixed up, then cover it close for half an hour, to let the flour stirred therein, be properly scalded, after which uncover and stir it frequently until it is a little colder than milk warm, (to be ascertained by holding your finger therein for ten minutes, but beware your finger is clean) then add half a pint of genuine good yeast,[1] (be certain it is good, for you had better use none, than bad yeast) and stir it effectually, until you are sure the yeast is perfectly incorporated with the ingredients in the pot—after which cover it, and set it in a moderately cool place in summer, until you perceive it begin to work, or ferment—then be careful to stir it two or three times at intervals of half an hour—then set it past to work—in the winter, place it in a moderately warm part of the still-house—and in summer, choose a spring house, almost up to the brim of the crock in water—avoiding extremes of heat or cold, which are equally prejudicial to the spirit of fermentation—of consequence, it should be placed in a moderately warm situation in the winter, and moderately cool in

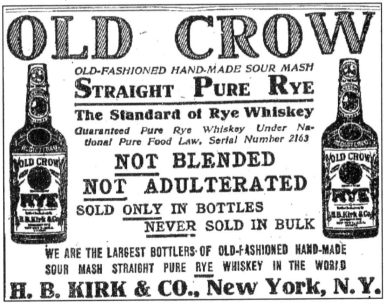

An advertisement for Old Crow that ran in the *New York Times* on New Year's Eve, 1909.

the summer.

This yeast ought to be renewed every four or five days in the summer, and eight or ten days in the winter—but it is safer to renew it oftener, or at shorter intervals, than suffering it to stand longer. In twenty-four hours after it begins to work, it is fit for use.

Between a pint and half a pint of the foregoing stock yeast, is sufficient to raise the yeast for the daily use of three hogsheads.

The most proper vessel for preserving stock yeast is an earthen crock, that will hold three gallons at least, with a cover of the same, well glazed—as it will contract no acid from the fermentation, and is easily scalded and sweetened. There ought to be two of the same size, that when one is in use, the other may be sweetening—which is effected by exposing them to frost or fire.

Wouldn't you know it—the first tax imposed by the United States federal government on a domestic product was a tax on whiskey. The brainchild of Alexander Hamilton, the tax was sought to pay off the new nation's debts after the Revolution. Distillers were taxed on the capacity of their stills, and required to pay this tax in cash. Oh the irony, as whiskey was the common monetary unit of the day.

It probably comes as no real surprise that the tax went over like a lead balloon. Many men refused to pay the tax, and those who came to collect were sometimes tarred and feathered.

TO KNOW WHEN YEAST IS GOOD OR BAD

When you perceive your yeast working, observe if it works quick, sharp and strong, and increasing in bulk nearly double what it was before it began to work, with a sweet sharp taste, and smell, with the appearance of a honey comb, with pores, and always changing place, with a bright lively color, then you may pronounce your yeast good; on the contrary, if it is dead, or flat and blue looking, with a sour taste, and smell, (if any at all,) then you may pronounce it bad, and unfit for use, and of course must be renewed.

HOW TO RENEW YEAST WHEN SOUR

About two hours before you begin to make your beer, take one pint of the sour yeast, put it into a clean dish or vessel, and pour clean cold water over it—changing the water every fifteen minutes, until the acid be extracted, have it then in readiness to mix with the beer, which is to be prepared, in the following manner, viz. Take one pint malt, and scald it well in a clean vessel, with a gallon of boiling water, let it stand half an hour closely covered—then pour it into a pot with plenty of hops—then strain it into a well scalded earthen jug, when milk warm—add then a small quantity of the yeast, (sweetened as directed in the first part of this receipt,) with two or three table spoonsful of molasses ... set it past for twenty four hours to ferment ... then

I HEART BOURBON

Mash Fermenter No. 7 at Buffalo Trace Distillery in Frankfort, KY, is one of 12 massive fermenters, each with a capacity of 92,000 gallons.

pour off the top, or beer that is in the jug, leaving about a quart in the bottom ... then that which remains in the bottom will be yeast with which to start your stock yeast.

The method of procuring and keeping stock yeast, by the generality of distillers, merits in the mind of the author of this work, most decided disapprobation. They generally procure yeast once a week, or month, from brewers, and if not convenient to be had in this way, they often use such as is used by country women, for baking bread, without paying any regard to the quality, or whether sour; with such, though generally bad, they proceed to make their daily yeast, and often continue the use of it, until the grain will no longer yield a gallon of whiskey to the bushel, and so often proceed in this miserable and indolent mode of procuring and renewing yeast, to the great prejudice of their own, and employer's interest ... attributing the small yield of liquor to the badness of the grain ... the manner in which it is chopped, or some other equally false cause. Then to the idle and careless habits of distillers, must be attributed any yield short of three gallons to the bushel of rye.... To ensure this quantity at least from the bushel, the author discovers the anxiety expressed, and the care recommended in the foregoing pages, on the subject of preserving and keeping good yeast, and recommends the following as the best mode of preparing.

STOCK YEAST GOOD FOR YEARS

When the weather is moderately warm in autumn or the spring, take of your best stock yeast that has fermented about twenty four hours, and stir it thick with the coarsest middlings of wheat flour, add small quantity of whiskey, in which, previously dissolve a little salt, when you have stirred the middlings with a stick, rub it between your hands until it becomes pretty dry, then spread it out thin, on a board to dry in the sun ... rubbing once or twice in the day between your hands until it is perfectly dry, which will be in three or four good days— taking it in at night before the dew falls—when it is properly dried, put it up in a paper and keep it in a dry airy place for use.

Thus yeast will keep good, if free from moisture, for any length of time, and it is the only effectual mode of preserving stock yeast pure and sweet ... when put up conformably to the foregoing instructions, the distiller may always rely on having it good, and depend on a good turn-out of his grain, provided he manages the other parts of his distilling equally well.

About two hours before you mean to use the dried yeast, the mode is to take two gills, place it in any convenient vessel, and pour thereon milk-warm water, stir and mix it well with the yeast, and in two or three hours good working yeast will be produced.

In the spring every distiller ought to make as much as would serve 'till fall, and every fall as much as will serve through the winter, reckoning on the use of one pint per week, three gills being sufficient to start as much stock yeast as will serve a common distillery one week.

KEEP YOUR **FRIENDS** CLOSE AND YOUR **BOURBON** CLOSER!

TO MAKE THE BEST YEAST FOR DAILY USE.

For three hogsheads take two handfuls of hops, put them into an iron pot, and pour thereon three gallons boiling water out of your boiler, set the pot on the fire closely covered half an hour, to extract the strength from the hops, then strain it into your yeast vessel, thicken it with chopped rye, from which the bran has been sifted ... stir it with a clean stick until the lumps are all well broken and mixed ... cover it close with a cloth for half an hour, adding at the time of putting in the chopped rye, one pint of good malt when the rye is sufficiently scalded, uncover and stir it well until it is milk-warm, then add one pint good stock yeast, stirring until you are sure it is well mixed with the new yeast. If your stock yeast is good, this method will serve you ... observing always, that your water and vessels are clean, and the ingredients of a good quality; as soon as you have cooled off and emptied your yeast vessel, scald and scour, and expose it to the night air to purify. Tin makes the best yeast vessel for yeast made daily, in the above mode.

In the course of my long practice in distilling I fully discovered that a nice attention to yeast is absolutely necessary, and although I have in the foregoing pages said a great deal on the subject, yet from the importance justly to be attached to this ingredient in distilling, and to shew more fully the advantages and disadvantages arising from the use of good and bad yeast, I submit the following statement for the consideration of my readers.

Advantages in using good yeast for one month, at 5 bushels per day;
30 days at 5 bushels, is 150 bushels at 60 cents costs   *$90*
150 bushels yield 3 gal/bushel at 50 cents/gal—450 gal   *$225*

Profit   *$135*
Disadvantages sustained during the above period:
150 bushels at 60 cents   *$90*
                                     Contra
150 bushels yielding 1 ½ gal/bushel—225 gal at
50 cents   *$112.50*
          Profit   *$21.50*

Thus the owner or distiller frequently sustains in the distillation of his produce, a loss, equal and in proportion to the foregoing—from the use of indifferent yeast, and often without knowing to what cause to attribute it. This statement will shew more forcibly, than any other mode—and is made very moderate on the side of indifferent yeast, for with bad sour yeast the yield will be oftener under one gallon to the bushel than above one and a half—whereas with good yeast the yield will rarely be so low as three gallons to the bushel. It is therefore, I endeavor so strongly to persuade the distiller to pay every possible attention to the foregoing instructions, and the constant use of good yeast only, to the total rejection of all which may be of doubtful quality.

In 1812, Elijah Pepper was practicing the art of distilling whiskey on the grounds that are currently home to Woodford Reserve. Its 500-foot-long barrel run is something to see, Woodford Reserve offers distillery tours as well as specialty sessions. For more information, check out their website at woodfordreserve.com.

Bourbon Pecan Balls

Submitted by Niki Drake

"I think about the three things I love when I make this recipe...my grandma, Kentucky & bourbon."

Ingredients
- 1 (16-ounce) package powdered sugar
- 1/3 cup bourbon
- 1/4 cup butter, softened
- 1 ¾ cups all-purpose flour
- 50 pecan halves (about 1 1/4 cups)

Chocolate Dip
- 2 cups semisweet chocolate morsels
- 1 tablespoon butter

Preheat oven to 350 degrees. In food processor or blender, process pecans with powdered sugar until finely ground. Set aside.

In large bowl cream butter and remaining sugar. Beat in vanilla. Add flour and ground pecans until blended. Roll dough into about 3 dozen walnut sized balls. Place 2" apart on ungreased cookie sheet. If balls or too sticky add a bit more powdered sugar or flour.

Bake 10-12 minutes or until lightly golden around edges. Place on wire rack to cool

Melt chocolate and butter in a saucepan over medium heat. Remove from heat. Dip bourbon balls in chocolate (coating whole or half) and place on wax paper.

Chill 1 hour or until hardened.

Chapter 2

OBSERVATIONS ON WOOD FOR HOGSHEADS

The cheapest and easiest wrought wood is generally most used for making mashing tubs, or hogsheads, and very often for dispatch or from necessity, any wood that is most convenient is taken, as pine or chestnut; indeed I have seen poplar tubs in use for mashing, which is very wrong, as a distiller by not having his hogsheads of good wood, may lose perhaps the price of two sets of hogsheads in one season. For instance, a farmer is about to erect a distillery, and is convenient to a mountain, abounding in chestnut or pine, which from its softness and the ease with which it may be worked, its convenience for dispatch sake, is readily chosen for his mashing hogsheads. To such selection of wood, I offer my most decided disapprobation, from my long experience, I know that any kind of soft wood will not do in warm weather. Soft porous wood made up into mashing tubs when full of beer and under fermentation, will contract, receive or soak in so much acid, as to penetrate nearly through the stave, and sour the vessel to such a degree, in warm weather, that no scalding will take it out—nor can it be completely sweetened until filled with cold water for two or three days, and then scalded; I therefore strongly recommend the use of, as most proper:

WHITE OAK

Disapproving of black, though next in order to white oak staves for all the vessels about the distillery ... as

Char on the Barrel. Traditionally speaking, bourbon barrels are charred to one of four levels of char. A No.1 Char is 15 seconds, a No.2 is 30; a No.3 Char is 35 seconds; and a No.4 Char is 55 seconds.

Also known as the "alligator char," the No.4 char produces a rough, shiny texture that looks like alligator skin on the inside of the oak barrel staves.

being the most durable of close texture, easily sweetened ... and hard to be penetrated by acids of any kind, though sometimes the best white oak hogsheads may sour, but two or three scaldings will render them perfectly sweet ... if white oak cannot

Barrel makers are referred to as coopers. It probably stands to reason that the term cooperage refers to companies that make barrels. ☺ Here in Kentucky, we go through a LOT of barrels.
Each new batch of bourbon must be placed a new charred white oak barrel.

be had, black oak being of the next best in quality may be used ... and again I enter my protest against pine, chestnut, poplar, and every kind of soft porous wood.

If possible, or if at all convenient, have the vessels iron bound and painted, to prevent worms and the weather from injuring them, using one good wood hoop on the bottom to save the chine.

TO SWEETEN HOGSHEADS BY SCALDING

When you turn your vessels out of doors (for it is esteemed slothful and a lazy mode to scald them in the still house,) you must wash them clean with your scrubbing brush, then put in sixteen or twenty gallons boiling water—cover it close for about twenty minutes, then scrub it out effectually with your scrubbing broom, then rinse your vessel well with a couple buckets clean cold water, and set them out to receive the air—this method will do in the winter, provided they are left out in the frost overnight—but in summer, and especially during the months of July and August, this mode will not do—it is during those extreme warm months in our latitude, that the vessels are liable to contract putrid particles, which may be corrected by the following mode of making hogsheads perfectly sweet.

Scald them twice, as above directed, then light a brimstone match, flick it on the ground, turn your hogshead down over it, let it stand until the match quits burning, this operation is necessary once a week—a method I have found effectual.

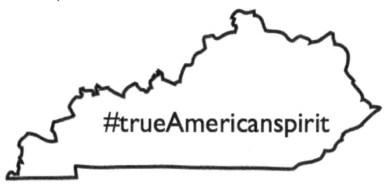

TO SWEETEN HOGSHEADS BY BURNING

When you have scalded your hogsheads well, put into each, a large handful of oat or rye straw, set it on fire, and stir it until it is in a blaze, then turn the mouth of the hogshead down; the smoke will purify and sweeten the cask. This process should be repeated every other day, especially during summer—it will afford you good working casks, provided your yeast be good, and your hogsheads are well mashed.

There ought always to be in a distillery more vessels than are necessary for immediate use, that they may alternately be exposed to the frost and air one night at least before brought into service, always bearing in mind that the utmost attention to cleanliness is necessary, in order to afford such yield from the grain, or fruit, as may be requisite to compensate for the expense and labor of extracting spirits—and moreover, that the exercise of the finest genius possessed by man is scarcely capable of taking from small grain, all the spirit it contains (good materials will not suffice) the most marked attentions indispensably necessary to yeast; a mind capable of judging of fermentation in all its stages ... a close adherence to the manner of using the ingredients ... preparing them, and the use of sweet vessels, with great industry and a knowledge to apply it at the proper moment, are all necessary to enable the accomplishment of the desired end. Note ... In scalding your hogshead I would recommend the use of a shovel full of ashes, which will scald more sharply.

The Heaven Hill Bourbon Heritage Center in Bardstown features this bourbon barrel chair and coordinating pillow near the facility's entry. You didn't expect anything less, did you? For more information, visit heavenhill.com.

WHISKEY SOUR

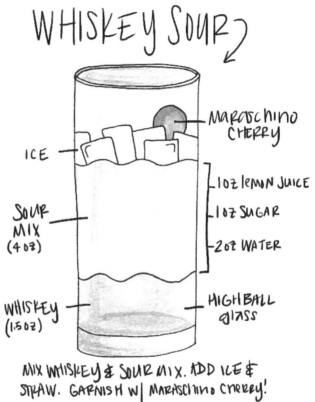

MARASCHINO CHERRY

ICE

1 OZ lemon JUICE

1 OZ SUGAR

2 OZ WATER

SOUR MIX (4 OZ)

WHISKEY (1.5 OZ)

HIGH BALL GLASS

MIX WHISKEY & SOUR MIX. ADD ICE & STRAW. GARNISH W/ MARASCHINO CHERRY!

Illustration courtesy of Kim Doughty, www.azulhome.com

Chapter 3

TO MASH RYE IN THE COMMON MODE

Take four gallons cold water to each hogshead, add one gallon malt, stir it well with your mashing stick, until the malt is thoroughly wet—when your still boils, put in about sixteen gallons boiling water, then put in one and an half bushels of chopped rye, stirring it effectually, until there is no lumps in it, then cover it close until the still boils, then put in each hogshead, three buckets or twelve gallons boiling water, stirring it well at the same time—cover it close—stir it at intervals until you perceive your rye is scalded enough, which will know by putting in your mashing stick, and lifting thereon some of the scalded rye, you will perceive the heart or seed of the rye, like a grain of timothy seed sticking to the stick, and no appearance of mush, when I presume it will be sufficiently scalded—it must then be stirred until the water is cold enough to cool off, or you may add one bucket or four gallons of cold water to each hogshead, to stop the scalding.

I have known this process succeed well with an attentive distiller.

THE BEST METHOD OF DISTILLING RYE

Take four gallons boiling, and two gallons cold water—put it into a hogshead, then stir in one and a half bushels chopped rye, let it stand five minutes, then add two gallons cold water, and one gallon malt, stir it effectually—let it stand until your still boils, then add sixteen gallons boiling water, stirring it well, or until you break all the lumps—then put into each hogshead, so prepared, one pint coarse salt, and one shovel full of hot coals out of your furnace. (The coals and salt have a tendency to absorb all sourness and bad smell, that may be in the hogshead or grain;) if there be a small quantity of hot ashes in the coals, it

Speaking of rye… Men and women—but especially women—are sometimes hesitant to try rye whiskeys, often because of a pre-existing bias. Those who don't like rye bread, for example, assume they won't like rye whiskey. But according to Dane Schlea, of Glenns Creek Distilling, you never know what you might be missing if you don't give it a taste. "Go in with an open mind," he said. "Don't be afraid to try new things!"

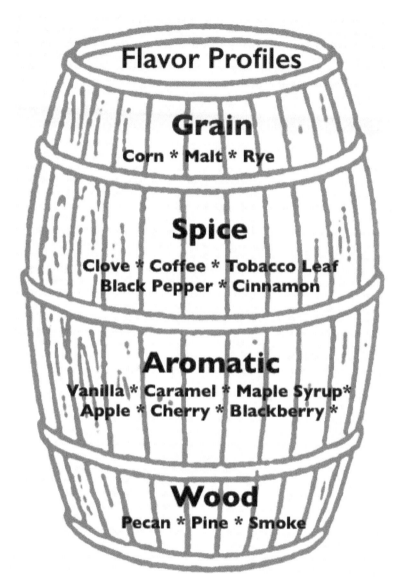

Flavor Profiles

Grain
Corn * Malt * Rye

Spice
Clove * Coffee * Tobacco Leaf
Black Pepper * Cinnamon

Aromatic
Vanilla * Caramel * Maple Syrup*
Apple * Cherry * Blackberry *

Wood
Pecan * Pine * Smoke

is an improvement—stir your hogsheads effectually every fifteen minutes, keeping them close covered until you perceive the grain scalded enough—when you may uncover, if the above sixteen gallons boiling water did not scald it sufficiently, water must be added until scalded enough—as some water will scald quicker than others—it is necessary to mark this attentively, and in mashing two or three times, it may be correctly ascertained what quantity of the kind of water used will scald effectually—after taking off the covers, they must be stirred effectually, every fifteen minutes, until you cool off—for which operation, see "*Cooling off.*" To those who distill all rye, I recommend this method, as I have found it to answer every kind of water, with one or two exceptions.

Distillers will doubtless make experiments of the various modes recommended and use that which may prove most advantageous and convenient.

TO MASH TWO THIRDS RYE AND ONE THIRD CORN IN SUMMER

This I have found to be the nicest process belonging to distilling—the small proportion of corn, and the large quantity of scalding water, together with the easy scalding of rye, and the difficulty of scalding corn, makes it no easy matter to exactly hit the scald of both; but as some distillers continue to practice it, (although not a good method in my mind, owing to the extreme nice attention necessary in performing it.) In the following receipt I offer the best mode within my knowledge, and which I deem the most beneficial, and in which I shew the process and mode pursued by other distillers.

Take four gallons cold water, put it into a hogshead, then stir half a bushel corn into it, let it stand uncovered thirty minutes, then add sixteen gallons boiling water, stir it well, cover it close for fifteen minutes, then put in your rye and malt and stir it until there be no lumps, then cover it and stir it at intervals until your still boils, then add, eight, twelve, or sixteen gallons boiling water, or such quantity as you find from experience, to answer best—(but with most water, twelve gallons will be found to answer) stirring it well every fifteen minutes until you perceive it is scalded enough, then uncover and stir it effectually until you cool off; keeping in mind always that the more effectually you stir it, the more whiskey will be yielded. This method I have found to answer best, however, I have known it to do very well, by soaking the corn in the first place, with two gallons warm, and two gallons cold water, instead of the four gallons of cold water, mentioned above—others put in the rye, when all the boiling water is in the hogshead, but I never found it to answer a good purpose, nor indeed did I ever find much profit in distilling rye and corn in this proportion.

#talkbourbontome

TO DISTILL ONE HALF RYE AND ONE HALF CORN

This method of distilling equal quantities of rye and corn, is more in practice, and is much better than to distill unequal proportions, for reason you can scald your corn and rye to a certainty, and the produce is equal if not more, and better whiskey, than all rye. The indian corn is cheaper, and the seed is better than if all rye. I would recommend this, as the smallest quantity of corn to be mixed with rye for distillation, as being

most productive, and profitable. The following receipt I have found to answer all waters—yet there may be places where the distiller cannot follow this receipt exactly, owing to hard or soft water, (as it is generally termed) or hard flint or soft floury corn, that will either scald too much or too little—but this the attentive distiller will soon determine by experience.

Have your hogshead perfectly sweet, put into each, three gallons of cold and three o boiling water, or more or less of each, as you find will answer best—then stir in your corn—fill up your boiler, bring it briskly to a boil—then put to each hogshead twelve gallons boiling water, giving each hogshead one hundred stirs, with your mashing stick, then cover close, fill up your boiler and keep a good fire under her, to produce a speedy boil; before you add the last water, put into each hogshead one pint of salt, and a shovel full of hot coals and ashes from under your still, stir the salt and coals well, to mix it with your corn, the coal will remove any bad smell which may be in the hogshead—Should

Here's a look at the sensory lab at Wild Turkey Distillery, where the whiskey is put to the test. Jimmy Russell and his son Eddie, who are the only active father/son bourbon master distillers in the world, are among the select few who enter this room. Learn more about Wild Turkey at wildturkeybourbon.com

SOUR MASH

The term "sour mash" refers to a process, not a flavor profile. Basically, the mash, which is a mixture of grain, malt, and water, gets a boost from a previously fermented, or spent batch of mash. Think of sourdough bread starters as an example of how the process works. Bottom line is that the method provides more consistency and quality from batch to batch.

you find on trial, that rye don't scald enough, by putting it in after your last water, you may in that case put in your rye before the last water—but this should be ascertained from several experiments. I have found it to answer best to put in the rye after all the water is in the hogshead, especially if you always bring the still briskly to a boil— then on your corn put twelve or sixteen gallons boiling water (for the last water) then if you have not already mashed in your rye, put it in with one gallon good malt to each hogshead, carefully stirring it immediately very briskly, for fear of the water losing its heat, and until the lumps are all broken, which you will discover by looking at your mashing stick; lumps generally stick to it. When done stirring, cover the hogshead close for half an hour, then stir it to ascertain whether your grain be sufficiently scalded, and when nearly scalded enough, uncover and stir steady until you have it cool enough to stop scalding; when you see it is scalded enough, and by stirring that the scalding is stopped, uncover your hogsheads, and stir them effectually, every fifteen minutes, until they are fit to cool off—remembering that sweet good yeast,

I'm here to kick ass and drink whiskey.
And Pilgrim, I'm out of whiskey.

clean sweet hogsheads, with this mode of mashing carefully, will produce you a good turn-out of your grain. The quantity of corn and rye is generally two stroked half bushels of each, and one-gallon malt.

TO MASH ONE THIRD RYE AND TWO THIRDS CORN

This I deem the most profitable mashing that a distiller can work, and if he can get completely in the way of working corn and rye in this proportion, he will find it
the easiest process of mashing. That corn has as much and as good whiskey as rye or any other grain, cannot be disputed, and

the slop or pot ale is much superior to that of any other grain, for feeding or fattening either horned cattle or hogs—one gallon of corn pot ale being esteemed worth three of rye, and cattle will always eat it better—and moreover, corn is always from one to two shillings per bushel cheaper than rye, and in many places much plentier—so that by adopting this method and performing it well, the distiller will find at the close of the year, it has advantages over all other processes and mixtures of rye and corn, yielding more profit, and sustaining the flock better. Hogs fatted on this pot ale, will be found decidedly better than any fatted on the slops of any other kind of mashing.

BOURBON.

...because no good story ever started with someone eating a salad.

MASH AS FOLLOWS

Have sweet hogsheads, good yeast and clean water in your boiler; when the water is sharp, warm, or half boiling, put into every hogshead you mean to mash at the same time, six, eight or as many gallons of the half boiling water, as will completely wet one bushel corn meal—add then one bushel chopped corn, stir it with your mashing stick until your corn is all wet; it is better to put in a less quantity of water first, and so add as you may find necessary, until completely wet (be careful in all mashings, that your mashing stick be clean) this is called soaking the corn. Then fill up your boiler, bring her quickly to a boil, when effectually boiling, put into every hogshead, twelve gallons boiling water, stirring it well after putting in each bucket, until the lumps are quite broken—cover the hogsheads close, after a complete stirring—fill up your boiler, bring her quickly to boil for the last mashing—stir the corn in the hogshead every fifteen minutes, until your last water is boiling—put into each hogshead one pint salt, and a shovel full of red hot coals, stirring it well—then put in each hogshead sixteen gallons of boiling water, stir it well— cover it close for twenty-five minutes—then put into each hogshead one half bushel rye meal, and one gallon good chopped malt, stirring it until the lumps are all broken, then cover it close, stir it every half hour, until you perceive it sufficiently scalded— then uncover it and stir it as often as your other business will permit, until ready to cool off.

In this and every other mashing you must use sweet vessels only and good yeast, or your labor will be in vain; and in all kinds of mashing you cannot stir too much.

TO MASH CORN

This is an unprofitable and unproductive mode of mashing, but there may be some times when the distiller is out of rye, on account of the mill being stopped, bad roads, bad weather, or some other cause; and to avoid the necessity of feeding raw grain to the hogs or cattle, (presuming every distillery to be depended on for supplying a stock of some kind, and often as a great reliance for a large stock of cattle and hogs,) in cold weather I have found it answer very well, but in warm weather it will not do. Those who may be compelled then from the above causes, or led to it by fancy, may try the following method. To one hogshead, put twelve gallons boiling water, and one and an half bushels corn, stir it well, then when your water boils, add twelve gallons more, (boiling hot,) stir it well, and cover it close, until the still boils the third time, then put in each hogshead, one quart of salt, and sixteen gallons boiling water, stir it effectually, cover it close until you perceive it nearly scalded enough, then put in two, or three gallons cold water (as you will find to answer best) and two gallons malt, or more if it can be spared—stir it well, then cover it for half an hour, then uncover and stir it well, until cold enough to cool off.

TO MAKE FOUR GALLONS FROM THE BUSHEL

This is a method of mashing that I much approve of, and recommend to all whiskey distillers to try it—it is easy in process, and is very little more trouble than the common method, and may be done in every way of mashing, as well with corn or rye, as also a mixture of each, for eight months in the year; and for the other four is worth the trouble of following. I do not mean to say that the quantity of four gallons can be made at an average,

Tony Davis not only produces Kentucky's first bourbon barrel-aged coffee, he's also "handcrafting the story of what Kentucky Knows through the barrel." His coffee beans sleep inside Buffalo Trace bourbon barrels, ultimately creating a product worthy of Kentucky's finest traditions. Next time you're in Frankfort, be sure to stop by his shop, have a cup of coffee, and ask him to tell you the story he discovered in the bourbon barrel. Put the Knows in your cup! Kentucky Knows is located at 337 West Broadway in Frankfort, KY. The website is kentuckyknows.com in every distillery, with every sort of grain, and water, or during every vicissitude of weather, and by every distiller, but this far I will venture to say, that a still house that is kept in complete order, with good water, grain well chopped, good malt, hops, and above all good yeast; together with an apt, careful and industrious distiller, cannot fail to produce at an average for eight months in the year, three and three quarter gallons from the bushel at a moderate calculation. I have known it sometimes produce four and a half gallons to the bushel, for two or three days, and sometimes for as many weeks, when perhaps, the third or fourth day, or week, it would scarcely yield three gallons; a change we must account for, in a change of weather, the water or the neglect or ignorance of the distiller. For instance, we know that four gallons of whiskey is in the bushel of rye or corn—certain, that this quantity has been made from the bushel; then why not always? Because, is the answer, there is something wrong, sour yeast or hogsheads, neglect of duty in the distiller, change of grain, or change of weather—then of course it is the duty of the distiller to guard against all these causes as near as he can. The following method, if it does not produce in every distillery the quantity above mentioned, will certainly produce more whiskey from the bushel, than any other mode I have ever known pursued.

Mash your grain in the method that you find will yield you most whiskey—the day before you intend mashing, have a clean hogshead set in a convenient part of the distillery; when your singling still is run off, take the head off and fill her up with clean water, let her stand half an hour, to let the thick part settle to the bottom, which it will do when settled, dip out with a gallon or pail, and fill the clean hogshead half full, let the hogshead stand until it cools a little, so that when you fill it up with cool water, it will be about milk-warm, then yeast it off with the yeast for

KENTUCKY HAS MORE BARRELS OF BOURBON THAN PEOPLE. COINCIDENCE?

making 4 gallons to the bushel, then cover it close, and let it work or ferment until the day following, when you are going to cool off; when the cold water is running into your hogshead of mashed stuff, take the one third of this hogshead to every hogshead, (the above being calculated for three hogsheads) to be mashed every day, stirring the hogsheads well before you yeast them off. This process is simple, and I flatter myself will be found worthy of the trouble.

TO KNOW WHEN GRAIN IS SCALDED ENOUGH

Put your mashing stick into your hogshead and stir it round two or three times gently, then lift it out and give it a gentle stroke on the edge of your hogshead—if you perceive the batter or musky part fall off your stick, and there remains the heart of the grain on your mashing stick, like grains of timothy seed, then be assured that it is sufficiently scalded, if not too much, this hint will suffice to the new beginner, but experience and observation will enable the most correct judgment.

DIRECTIONS FOR COOLING OFF

Much observation is necessary to enable the distiller to cool off with judgment—which necessity is increased by the versatility of our climate, the seasons of the year, and the kinds of water used. These circumstances prevent a strict adherence to any particular or specific mode; I however submit a few observations for the guidance of distillers in this branch. If in summer you go to cool off with cold spring water, then of course the mashed stuff in your hogsheads must be much warmer, than if you intended cooling off with creek or river water, both of which are generally near milk warm, which is the proper heat for cooling off—In summer a little cooler, and in winter a little warmer.

It will be found that a hogshead of mashed grain will always get warmer, after it begins to work or ferment.

When the mashed stuff in your hogsheads is brought to a certain degree of heat, by stirring, which in summer will feel sharp warm, or so warm, that you can hardly bear your hand in it for any length of time, will do for common water, but for very cold or very warm water to cool off with, the stuff in the hogsheads must be left colder or warmer, as the distiller may think most expedient, or to best suit the cooling off water.

When you think it is time to cool off, have a trough or conveyance to bring the water to your hogsheads ready—let the hogsheads be well stirred, then let the water run into them slowly, stirring them all the time the water is running in, until they are milk warm, then stop the water, and after stirring them perfectly, put in the yeast and stir it until completely incorporated with the mashed stuff, then cover your hogshead until it begins to ferment or work, then uncover it.

TO ASCERTAIN WHEN RYE WORKS WELL IN THE HOGSHEAD

When mashed rye begins to work or ferment in the hogsheads, either in a heavy, thick, or light bubbly top, both of which are unfavorable; when it rises in a thick heavy top, you may be sure there is something wrong, either in the grain, yeast, or cooling off. When the top (as called by distillers) appear, with bubbles about the size of a nutmeg, rising and falling alternately, with the top not too thick nor too thin, and with the appearance of waves, mixed with the grain in the hogshead, rising and falling in succession, and when you put your head over the steam, and it flying into your nose, will have a suffocating effect, or when it will instantly extinguish a candle when held over it, you may feel assured, it is working well.

From these hints and the experience of the distiller, a judgment may be formed of the state of fermentation and the quality.

It turns out Kentucky's farm animals are direct recipients of the bourbon industry. They feast on all the leftovers, known as distiller's grain, or slop (as it is lovingly referred to), which is high in protein, fat and fiber. Is it any wonder we have such happy cows?

TO PREVENT HOGSHEADS FROM WORKING OVER

If the stuff is cooled off too warm, or too much yeast is put in the hogsheads, they will work over, and of course lose a great deal of spirit, to prevent which, take tallow and rub round the chine of the hogsheads a little higher than they ought to work; it will generally prevent them from rising any higher, but if they will work over in spite of this remedy, then drop a little tallow into the stuff, it will immediately sink the stuff to a proper height.

Here in the Bluegrass State, climate, conditions and pure limestone combine to make the world's best bourbon. #matchmadeinHeaven

Mr. Food's Whiskey Cake

Submitted by Shirley Earlywine Willoughby

"I'd seen Mr. Food on television one year and decided to make this cake," Shirley said. *"Now I make it for Christmas and the occasional family reunion. There's never any left to bring home."*

1 pkg. yellow cake mix
 (batter prepared according to box directions)
1/2 cup chopped pecans
1 tsp all-purpose flour
1/4 cup butter
1/2 cup sugar
1/2 cup whiskey (namely bourbon! hello!)

Preheat oven to 350. Coat a bunt pan with nonstick spray. In a small bowl, combine pecans and flour; mix well until pecans are well coated. Stir nuts into cake batter. Pour batter into pan and bake 35 minutes or until cake tester comes out clean.

In small saucepan, combine whiskey, sugar and butter and bring to a boil over medium-high heat. Let boil 5 minutes, stirring occasionally. Using a fork, poke holes all over the top of the cake. Pour syrup over cake. Let cake set for 15 minutes then remove to wire rack.

Chapter 4

OBSERVATIONS ON THE QUALITY OF RYE FOR DISTILLING

The best rye for distilling is that which is thoroughly ripe, before it is cut, and kept dry until threshed; if it has grown on high or hilly ground, it is therefore to be preferred, being then sounder and the grain fuller, than that produced on low level land—but very often the distiller has no choice, but must take that which is most convenient;—great care however ought to be observed in selecting sound rye, that has been kept dry, is clean and free from cockle, and all kind of dirt, advantages will result from fanning it, or running it through a windmill before it is chopped.

MODE OF CHOPPING RYE AND THE PROPER SIZE

The mill stones ought to be burrs, and kept very sharp for

Leaving a Trail

As whiskey ages, a small amount of ethanol evaporates from the barrel, providing the perfect breeding ground for whiskey fungus. This naturally occurring fungus runs rampant at distillery locations, covering everything in the immediate environment (trees, buildings, etc.) with a black gunk. Back in the day, it was a tell-tale sign of moonshiner activity.

chopping rye for distillation; and the miller ought to be careful not to draw more water on the wheel than just sufficient to do it well, and avoid feeding the stones plentifully; because in drawing a plentiful supply of water, the wheel will compel a too rapid movement of the stones, of course render it necessary they should be more abundantly fed, which causes part to be ground dead, or too fine, whilst part thereof will be too coarse, and not sufficiently broken, so that a difficulty arises in scalding—for in this state it will not scald equally, and of consequence, the fermentation cannot be so good or regular; and moreover as part of it will merely be flattened, a greater difficulty will arise in breaking the lumps, when you mash and stir your hogsheads. If burr stones are very sharp, I recommend the rye to be chopped very fine, but to guard against over-seeding, or pressing too much on them; but if the stones are not sharp, I would recommend the rye should be chopped about half fine. Distillers in general sustain a loss from having their rye chopped so coarse as I have observed it done in common.

CHOPPING OR GRINDING INDIAN CORN

Indian corn cannot be ground too fine for distilling.

MALT

Cannot be ground too coarse, provided it is done even— there ought to be no fine nor coarse grains in malt, but ground perfectly alike, and of the same grade. If ground too fine, it will be apt to be scalded too much in mashing. Malt does not require half the scalding necessary in rye. Let the distiller try the experiment of coarse and then of fine ground malt and judge for himself.

HOW TO CHOOSE MALT

Malt is chosen by its sweet smell, mellow taste, full flower, round body and thin skin. There are two kinds used, the pale and

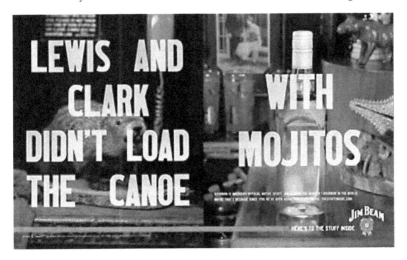

Some things need no explanation, like this magazine ad from Jim Beam. The brand was named in honor of James B. Beam, who rebuilt the business after Prohibition ended in 1933. Find out more at jimbeam.com.

the brown—the pale is the best.

HOW TO BUILD A MALT KILN IN EVERY DISTILLERY

When setting up your stills, leave a space of about nine inches for a small furnace between the large ones, extend it to your chimney and carry up a funnel, there—from to the loft, then stop it—here build the kiln on the loft, about 4 or 5 feet square, the walls to be composed of single brick, 3 feet high—lay the bottom with brick, cover it with a plaster of mortar, to prevent the floor from taking fire. Turn the funnel of the chimney into, and extend it to the center of the kiln, cover the top, leaving vent holes at the sides for the heat to escape through—Place on the top of the kiln, sheet iron or tin punched full of small holes, too small to admit the passage of malt; lay the malt on the top of the tin, when ready for drying. Put coals from under the still furnace into the small furnace leading to the kiln, which will heat the kiln and dry the malt above, by adding to or diminishing the quantity of coals, the heat may be increased or decreased, as may be found necessary. Malt for distilling ought to be dried without smoke.

HOPS

Give a preference to hops of a bright green color, sweet smell, and have a gummy or clammy effect when rubbed between the hands or fingers.

I'm hoping at this point that y'all are ready to head to the closest distillery ASAP. If so (and we both know it's true) you've got to hook up with the Kentucky Bourbon Boys! This group of lifelong Kentuckians (9 guys and a gal) have been taking people on bourbon tours for a number of years, now, offering transportation to and from select distilleries (and a little lunch in between). They'll even pick you up if you want!

It should come as no surprise that bourbon distillers crop up in the Kentucky Bourbon Boys' family trees, starting with Tim Hagan, whose mother's great, great grandfather was JW Dant's brother — JW was widely reputed for making his whiskey in a log still. "There are Willetts, Wathens, and Thompsons in our genealogy too," Tim said.

Their tours are a great way to celebrate with friends, plan an outing for out-of-state company, or simply enjoy a day with like-minded folks. As the Kentucky Bourbon Boys say, a combination of good friends and good bourbon adds up to an uncommon wealth.

Be sure to check them out at kentuckybourbonboys.com, find them on social media: @KYBourbonBoys on Twitter and Instagram, and on Facebook at Kentucky Bourbon Boys.

Bourbon Butter Sauce
Submitted by Elaine Smalling-Perkins

1/2 cup butter
1 cup sugar
1 egg, well beaten
1/4 cup bourbon

Melt butter in saucepan and add sugar. Heat to dissolve. Remove from heat and blend egg into hot butter mixture. Whisk in bourbon and heat briefly to a smooth, creamy consistency that coats the back of a spoon. (Do not simmer as mixture will curdle.)

Serve warm over bread pudding, cake, ice cream or fresh fruit.

Some have questioned if one can bathe in Bourbon Butter Sauce. The answer of course is that you can, but the real question (if you'd like to keep up the appearances of being a true southern belle or gentleman) is whether you should. ☺

In 1964, the United States Congress Proclaimed Bourbon as America's Only Native Spirit.

Chapter 5

HOW TO ORDER AND FILL THE SINGLING STILL WHEN DISTILLING RYE.

Scrape, clean, and grease the singling still, fill her up with beer, and keep a good fire under her until she be warm enough to head, stirring her constantly with a broom,

to prevent the grain from sticking to the bottom or sides, and burning, which it is very apt to do when the beer is cold, but when it comes to boil there is little danger, prevented by the motion of boiling; have the head washed clean—when she is ready for the head, clap it on and paste it; keep up a brisk fire, until she begins to drop from the worm, then put in the damper in the chimney, and if the fire be very strong, moderate it a little, by throwing ashes or water on it, to prevent her throwing the head, which she will be very apt to do if very full, and coming round under a strong fire, (should the head come, or be thrown

Town Branch Distillery in Lexington is one piece of the Alltech Brewing and Distilling Company, which also produces ale (including a bourbon barrel ale). For hours of operation and tours (which include brewing and distilling!) visit Kentucky ale.com.

off, the spirit remaining will scarcely be worth running off). When fairly round and running moderately, watch her for half an hour; after which, unless the fire is very strong all danger is over.

Should she happen to throw the head, it is the duty of the distiller to take and (wash the head and worm—the latter will be found full of stuff) clean, clap on the head, and paste it—but the moment the head is thrown off, the fire should be drowned out, and water thrown into the still to prevent her boiling over.

It is important that after every run, or rather before you

commence a run, the distiller should carefully clean out the still, wipe the bottom dry, and grease her well, to prevent her from burning and singeing the liquor.

MODE OF MANAGING THE DOUBLING STILL WHEN MAKING WHISKEY

Let the doubling still be carefully cleaned and washed out, then be filled with singlings and low wines left from the run preceding, add thereto half a pint of salt and one quart of clean ashes, which will help to clear the whiskey, and a handful of Indian meal to prevent the still from leaking at the cock, or elsewhere—clean the head and worm, put on the head, paste it well; put fire under and bring her round slowly, and run the spirit off as slow as possible, and preserve the water in the cooling tub as cold as in your power.

Let the liquor as it runs from the worm pass through a flannel to prevent the overjuice from the copper, and the oil of the grain from mixing with the spirit. The first being poisonous, and the latter injurious to the liquor.

#TGIB*
*Thank God it's Bourbon!

The doubling still cannot be run too slow for making good whiskey ... observe when the proof leaves the worm, that is when there is no proof on the liquor as it comes from the worm, if there be ten gallons in your doubling keg, if so, run out three more, which will make in all thirteen gallons first proof whiskey. If the proof leaves the worm at eight gallons, then run until eleven gallons and so on in proportion, to the larger or smaller quantity in your keg at the time of the ceasing of the proof.

> "Always carry a flagon of whiskey in case of snakebite, and furthermore always carry a small snake."
>
> —W.C. Fields

OBSERVATIONS ON THE ADVANTAGES OF MAKING STRONG AND GOOD WHISKEY WITH STALEMENT, ETC.

The distiller who makes whiskey for a market under the government of inspection laws, too weak, sustains a loss of a cent for each degree it may be under proof ... and the disadvantages are increased in proportion to the extent of land carriage. If a distance of seventy miles, the price of carriage per gallon will be about six cents, paying the same price for weak or strong ... not only the disadvantage of paying for the carriage of feints or water, but the loss in the casks, which though small apparently at first view, yet if nicely attended to, will amount in the course of the year to a sum of moment to every distiller or proprietor. To convey my ideas, or render a more complete exposition of my impressions as to the actual loss on one wagon load (predicated on a distance of seventy miles land carriage) of first proof whiskey, and that nine degrees under proof. I give the following statement.

300 gallons good first proof whiskey at 50 cents	$150
hauling at six cents	$ 18
total	$132

300 gallons whiskey nine degrees under proof	$123
at 41 cents, hauling?	$ 18
total	
	$105
Difference (between totals)	$ 27

This difference of twenty-seven dollars in favor of the distiller, who sends first proof whiskey, is not the only advantage, but he saves in barrels or casks, what will contain fifty-four gallons, nearly two barrels; which together with the time saved, or gained in running good whiskey only, of filling and measuring it out, loading, etc.. will leave an advantage of I presume, three dollars in each load. Or to verify more satisfactorily, and I hope my readers will not think me too prolix, as economy cannot be too much attended to in this business, I add a statement predicated on a year's work, and on the foregoing principles:

The distiller of weak whiskey, in twelve months, or one year, distils at the rate of 100 gallons per week—or say in the year, he prepares for a market at the above distance, 5000 gallons, which ought to command $2,500.

But he sustains a loss or deduction of 9 cents, or $450. Then the first loss may safely be computed at $450.

150 empty barrels necessary to contain 5000 gallons, at 33 1/3 gallons to the barrel, estimating the barrel at 7s and 6d, is $150.

This quantity of whiskey, when reduced to proof, is 4,100 gals. which would have occupied only 123 barrels, 123 from 150 is 27.

Then the second loss may be estimated at $27.

Everybody loves a redhead.

He ought to have made this quantity of 4,100 gallons in nine months and three weeks, but we will say 10 months, sustaining a loss of two months in the year:

3d item of loss: Hire of distiller for 2 months at $12 equals $24 00.

4th do. Rent of distillery do. at £15 per annum._ $ 6.66

5th do. One sixth of the wood consumed, (at the rate of 100 cords per annum,) equals 16 cords, $20

6th do. One sixth of the Malt, do. say 90 bushels, is $90

7th do. Is the wear and tear of stills, vessels, &c. $12.34 Total Loss:

$ 630

Showing hereby a total annual loss to the careless distiller, of six hundred and thirty dollars, and a weekly loss of twelve dollars and three cents in the whiskey of nine degrees below proof—our ninth part of which is seventy dollars, which is the sum of loss sustained on each degree in this quantity of whiskey.

The foregoing I flatter myself will not only show the necessity of care, cleanliness, industry and judgment, in the business of distilling; a business professed to be known, by almost everybody—but in reality quite a science, and so abstruse as to be but too imperfectly understood; and moreover, the value of time, so inestimable in itself, the economy of which is so rarely attended to.

DISTILLING OF BUCKWHEAT

Buckwheat is an unprofitable grain for the distillers when distilled by itself, but when mixed with rye, it will yield nearly as much as rye; but I would by no means recommend the use of it when it can be avoided. Though sometimes necessity requires that a distiller should mash it for a day or two, when anything is the matter, or that grain cannot be procured. In such event, the directions for distilling rye, or rye and corn may be followed, but it requires a much larger quantity of boiling water and if distilled by itself; it is necessary some wheat bran be mixed with it to raise it to the top of the hogshead: but by no means use buckwheat meal in making yeast.

DISTILLING OF POTATOES

This is a branch of distilling that I cannot too highly recommend to the attention of every American—nor can the cultivation of this valuable vegetable be carried to a too great extent, the value of which ought to be known to every planter and it sometimes has awakened my surprise that they are not more cultivated, as it is notorious that they will sustain, and be a

During the days of Prohibition, the only (legal) way to get your hands on a drink was with a doctor's prescription. Buffalo Trace was one of four distilleries—and the only distillery in Kentucky—permitted to operate between 1920 and 1933. Because whiskey was good for whatever ailed people, some were sick for 13 straight years! ☺

tolerable food for everything possessing life on this earth—and as they produce a brandy, if properly made, of fine flavour. I hope yet to see the day when it will take precedence of French brandy and West-India spirits, and thereby retain in our own country, the immense sums at present expended on those foreign liquors; which, though benefitted by the sea voyage, yet often reaches us in a most pernicious state, and is frequently adulterated here.

Could the American farmer be brought to raise a larger quantity of potatoes than necessary for his consumption at home, the price would be lowered, and the distiller might commence the distillation of them with greater propriety. That they contain a great deal and a very good spirit, I am certain, and moreover, after distillation will yield as great a quantity of good wholesome food for cattle or hogs, as rye or any other grain. If distillers could be brought to try the experiment of distilling ten or twelve bushels annually, I venture to predict that it would soon become a source of profit to themselves, encouragement to the farmer, and be of benefit to our country at large.

One acre of ground, if well farmed, will produce from fifty to one hundred bushels of potatoes, but say sixty on an average. One hundred farmers each planting one acre, would yield six thousand bushels, which will yield at least two gallons of spirit to each bushel; thus, twelve thousand gallons of wholesome spirit may be produced, and with care, as good as necessary to be drank. Each farmer proceeding in this way, would have one hundred and twenty gallons spirit, as much as he may have occasion to use in the year, which would save the price of some acres of wheat or one hundred and twenty gallons rye whiskey. Each acre worked in potatoes will be in better order to receive a crop of wheat, barley, rye, or any kind of grain, than from any other culture. The farmer often receiving the advantage of a double crop, at the expense of seed and labor. They grow equally well in every soil and climate, in poor as well as rich ground—provided the thin soil be manured, and the potatoes plastered with plaster of Paris; and moreover, they are easier prepared for distilling than either apples, rye or corn, as I shall show hereafter when I come to treat of the mode of preparation; and in order to demonstrate the advantages that would arise to the farmer and distiller; I add a statement of the probable profits of ten acres of potatoes, and that of a like number of acres of rye, to shew which offers the greatest advantages.

Potatoes:
Ten acres at 60 bushels per acre is 600 bushels at 33 cents
  $198
Rye:
Ten acres at 30 bushels per acre, is 300 bushels at 60 cents

$180

CR.

600 bushels yielding 2 gallons to the bushel, 1,200 gallons at 50
cents   is $600 $402

CR.

300 bushels yielding 3 gallons to the bushel, 900 gallons at 50 cents
or $450. $270

Balance in favor of potatoes $132

Thus a balance of $132 would appear in favor of the yield of potatoes.

I would not pretend to say that ten acres of Potatoes will not take more labor than ten acres of rye, but this far I will venture to say, that the profits arising from the sale of this brandy, will more than double pay the additional expense of raising them, besides the ground will be in much better condition to receive a crop of wheat, than the rye ground, nay, will be enriched from the crop, whilst the rye ground will be greatly impoverished.

RECEIPT TO PREPARE POTATOES FOR DISTILLING.

Wash them clean, and grind them in an apple mill, and if there be no apple mill convenient, they may be scalded and then pounded—then put two or three bushels into a hogshead and fill the hogshead nearly full of boiling water, and stir it well for half an hour, then cover it close until the potatoes are scalded quite soft, then stir them often until they are quite cold—then put into each hogshead about two quarts of good yeast and let them ferment, which will require eight or ten days—the beer then may be drawn off and distilled, or put the pulp and all into the still, and distill them as you do apples. I have known potatoes distilled

Photo courtesy of Liz Wright

Once the bourbon leaves the belly of the barrel, other spirits, including rum, scotch, wine and beer, often find their way in. Even herbs and spices are known to get an extra kick from doing time in the barrel. Kentucky Bourbon Barrel Ale also ages in a freshly decanted barrel, and is a staple in this author's refrigerator,. Who can say #bourbonbeer?

> "The water was not fit to drink. To make it palatable, we had to add whisky. By diligent effort, I learned to like it."
>
> —Winston Churchill

in this way to yield upwards of three gallons to the bushel.

PUMPKINS AND TURNIPS

May be prepared by the same process used in preparing potatoes, with the exception of not scalding them so high, nor do they require so much yeast.

Turnips will produce nearly as much spirit as potatoes, but not so good. They must be prepared in the same manner.

HOW TO DISTILL APPLES

Apples ought to be perfectly ripe for distillation, as it has been ascertained from repeated trials, that they produce more and better spirit, (as well as cider), when fully ripe than if taken green, or the ripe and unripe mixed—if taken mixed it will not be found practicable to grind them evenly, or equally fine; those fully ripe will be well ground, whilst those hard and unripe will be little more than broken or slightly bruised—and when this coarse and fine mixture is put into a hogshead to work or ferment, that fully ripe and fine ground, will immediately begin, and will be nearly if not quite done working before the other begins, and of course nearly all the spirit contained in the unripe fruit will be lost—and if it is left standing until the ill ground unripe fruit is thoroughly fermented, and done working, you will perceive that a large portion of the spirit contained in the ripe well ground fruit is evaporated and of course lost.

But if the fruit be all ripe and evenly ground, of course then it will work regularly and can be distilled in due and right order, and will produce the greatest quantity of spirit, and much superior to that produced from uneven, ill-ground or unripe fruit. Apples cannot be ground too fine.

HOW TO ORDER APPLES IN THE HOGSHEADS

When the apples are ground put them into open hogsheads to ferment, taking care not to fill them too full, or they will work over; set them under cover, as the sun will sour them too soon, if permitted to operate on them, and by his heat extract a considerable quantity of the spirit, if the weather be warm they will work fast enough, provided you have a sufficient supply of hogsheads to keep your stills going in due time and order; about twenty hogsheads are sufficient to keep one singling still of one hundred and ten gallons going, if you distil the pumice with the juice, but if you press off the apples after they are done working, you must have three times that number. In warm weather five or six days is long enough for apples to work, as it is always better to distil them before they are quite done working, then to let them stand one hour after the fermentation ceases.

HOW TO WORK APPLES SLOW OR FAST

If the hogsheads ripens too fast for your stills, add every day to each hogshead four gallons cold spring water, putting it into a hole made in the center of the apples, with a large round stick of wood; by thus putting it into the center of the hogshead, it will chill the fermentation, and thereby prevent the fruit from becoming ripe sooner than it may suit the convenience of the distiller. But I think it advisable that distillers should take in no more apples than they can properly manage in due time. If the weather be cold, and the apples do not ripen so fast as you wish, then add every twelve hours, four gallons boiling, or warm water, which will ripen them if the weather be not too cold in four days at farthest.

These days, even the world of digital technology is on board the bourbon train. Podcasts make it easier than ever to gain an informal education and stay up to date on the latest news and stories about all things bourbon. Here are a few good ones to get you started:

- American Whiskey Podcast
- Bourbon Pursuit
- Bottom of the Barrel
- Sips, Suds, and Smokes
- Modern Thirst

Photo courtesy of Wilderness Trail Distillery

Wilderness Trail Distillery founders Pat Heist and Shane Baker craft vodka, rum, and of course, bourbon at their distillery, the oldest in Danville, Kentucky. When it comes to stressing the importance of bourbon in the Commonwealth, they like to quote Parker Beam, Master Distiller for Heaven Hill: "You can make bourbon anywhere in the US, but if you want to sell it, it better damn well be made in Kentucky." Check out these guys at wildernesstraildistillery.com.

HOW TO JUDGE WHEN APPLES ARE READY FOR DISTILLING

Put your hand down into the hogsheads amongst the apples as far as you can, and bring out a handful of pugs— squeeze them in your hand, through your fingers, observe if there be any core, or lumps of apples undigested, if none, you may consider them as sufficiently fermented and quite ready for distilling. It may also be ascertained by tasting and smelling the cider or juice, which rises in the hole placed in the center; if it tastes sweet and smells strong, it is not yet ready, but when quite fermented, the taste will be sour, and smell strong, which is the proper taste for distilling. A nice discriminating attention is necessary to ascertain precisely, when the fermentation ceases, which is the proper moment for distillation, and I would recommend, rather to anticipate, than delay one hour after this period.

HOW TO FILL AND ORDER THE SINGLING STILL, WHEN RUNNING APPLE SINGLINGS

When you perceive your apples ready for distilling, fill the singling still with apples and water; using about half a hogshead apples in a still of 110 gallons, the residue water, first having cleaned the still well, and greased her previous to filling—put fire under her and bring her ready to head, as quick as possible, stirring the contents well with a broom until ready to head, of which you can judge by the warmth of the apples and water, which must be rather warm to bear your hand in it any length of time. Wash the still head and worm clean, put on the head, paste it, keeping a good fire until she runs at the worm; run off 14 gallons briskly, and catch the feints in a bucket to throw into the next still full, if the singling still too fast, provided she does not smoke at the worm. When the first still full is off, and before you go to fill her the second time, draw or spread the coals that may be under her, in the furnace, and fill the furnace with wood. Shut up your furnace door and put in your damper; by proceeding thus, you cool the still and avoid burning her; this plan I deem preferable to watering out the fire. When empty, rinse the still

"If she were a drink, she'd be a single barrel bourbon on ice. Smooth with a kick, a chill, and a burn all at the same time."
—Brad Paisley

round with cold water, scrape and grease her, then she will be ready to receive a second charge. Care is necessary in scraping and greasing your still every time she is emptied, if this is neglected, the brandy may be burnt and the still injured.

HOW TO DOUBLE APPLE BRANDY.
Fill the doubling still with singlings, and add a quart of lime, (which will clear it) put fire under her and bring her to a run briskly—after she runs, lessen the fire and run her as slow as possible. Slow running will prevent any of the spirit from escaping, and make more and better brandy, than fast running. Let the liquor filter through a flannel cloth from the worm.

HOW TO PREPARE PEACHES
Peaches like apples ought to be equally ripe, in order to insure an equal and regular fermentation—for where ripe and unripe fruit are thrown into the same hogshead, and ordered for distillation in this way a disadvantage is sustained. I therefore recommend to farmers and distillers, when picking the peaches to assort them when putting them in hogsheads, all soft ripe peaches may go together, as also those which are hard and less ripe—this will enable a more regular fermentation, and though the hard and less ripe, will take a longer time, than the soft and ripe to ferment, and yield less, yet the disadvantage will not be so great, as if mixed.

They ought to be ground in a mill with metal nuts, that the stone and kernel may be well broken. The kernel when thus broken will give a finer flavor to the brandy, and increase the quantity. When they are ground they must be placed in hogsheads and worked in the same way with apples, but distilled sooner or they will lose much more spirit by standing any time after fermentation than apples. It is therefore better to distil them a short time before they are done working than at any period after.

NOTE: The same process must be observed in running off peaches as in apples, except that the singling still ought not to be run so fast, nor so much fire kept under her, and more water used to prevent burning.

Speaking of single barrel bourbon... this is probably a good time to talk about some terms associated with our new best friend.

Single Barrel means that the bourbon has been bottled from one single barrel. In other words, that bourbon spent its whole life in the same barrel, and never intermingled with other barrels.

Small Batch Bourbon: When those big barrels go off to the rick houses to age, the end flavor depends on where that barrel rested—a barrel on the top floor will have a different profile from one on the bottom floor for example. So a small batch bourbon will mingle select barrels for a specific flavor profile.

Straight Bourbon: This designation means the bourbon has been aged at least two years. If it's older than two, but younger than four years old, the label must reflect the age. If it's over four years old, no age statement is required.

Bacon Bourbon Meatballs
Submitted by Marsha Hunt

Marsha Hunt is one of America's Gold Star Mothers. Her son Joey was killed in Iraq in 2005. Joey loved to eat—it was a hobby of sorts. So in honor of Joey, Marsha passed along this tried and true recipe.

6 strips of bacon
½ medium onion
1 lb ground beef
½ c. breadcrumbs
2 T fresh chopped parsley
1 large egg
1 tsp chili powder
1 tsp salt
1 T vegetable oil
1 c barbeque sauce
½ cup water
3T bourbon

Place uncooked bacon into a food processor and process for 1 minute or until bacon is finely ground. Repeat process with onion. Place in bowl and add beef, breadcrumbs, parsley, egg and spices. Still well. Form into about 24 1-inch balls.

Heat oil in skillet over medium hit and brown meatballs on all sides, about 10 minutes. Remove and drain grease out of pan. Add bourbon, water and barbeque sauce to pan and heat. Once heated, add meatballs and simmer for at least 15 minutes.

Chapter 6

THE BEST METHOD OF SETTING STILLS

If stills are not set right, great injury may accrue to them, in burning and damaging the sides, singeing the whiskey, and wasting of fuel too, are not the only disadvantages; but more damage may be done in six months, than would pay a man of judgment for putting up twenty pair.

If they are set with their bottoms to the fire, they are very apt to burn, without the utmost care of the distiller, in stirring her when newly filled with cold beer, until she is warm, and by previously greasing the bottom well when empty. If wood be plenty, stills ought to be set on an arch, but if scarce, the bottom ought to be set to the fire. The following method is calculated for a furnace of either two or four feet long, and with the bottoms exposed, or on an arch as the distiller may fancy.

The Seven Standards of Distilling Bourbon

1. Must be put in a new American White Oak charred barrel.
2. Must be made in the USA.
3. Mash build must be 51 percent corn. The remaining 49 percent can be another grain, such as rye, barley, wheat or even additional corn.
4. Cannot be distilled at more than 160 proof.
5. Cannot be barreled at more than 125 proof.
6. Cannot be bottled at less than 80 proof.
7. No additives may be used to change the flavor or color.

Make up a quantity of well worked mortar, composed of the greater proportion of good clay, a little lime and cut straw.

Lay the bottom of the furnace with flag stones, or good brick, from two to four feet long, as may be deemed most proper, let it be from twelve to sixteen inches wide, and from twelve to fourteen high. Then if it is designed to turn an arch, set the end of a brick on each wall of the furnace, leaning them over the furnace, until they meet in the middle—so continue the range on each side, until the furnace is completely covered in, leaving a small hole for the flue leading to the chimney behind, leaning towards the side, from which the flue is to be started, to proceed round the bilge of the still, which passage must be ten by four inches wide.

After completing the arch as described, lay thereon a

> *"I have never in my life seen a Kentuckian who didn't have a gun, a pack of cards, and a jug of whiskey."*
>
> —Andrew Jackson,
> 7th President of the United States

complete bed of mortar, well mixed with cut straw, se t the still thereon, levelling her so that she will nearly empty herself by the stoop towards the cock; then fill up all round her with mortar to the lower rivets, carefully preventing any stone or brick from touching her, (as they would tend to burn her) ... then build the fender or fenders; being a wall composed of brickbats and clay well mixed with cut straw, build it from the commencement of the flue, and continue it about half round the still ... this is to prevent the flames from striking the still sides, in its hot state, immediately after it leaves the furnace, presuming that it will terminate before it reaches the end of this little wall or fender, between which, and the still, a space of two inches ought to be left for the action of the heat, which space preserves, and prevents the wall or fender, from burning the still; the mode in common practice, being to place it against the still, which will certainly singe or burn her. When this defender is finished, commence a wall, which continue round, laying a brick for a foundation, about four inches from the lower rivets; thus raising this wall for the flue, continuing it at an equal distance from the still, leaving a concave to correspond with the bilge of the still, and to be of precisely the same width and height all round the still. This precaution is absolutely necessary in building the wall of the flue exactly to correspond with the form of the still, and equally distant all round, for reasons 1st. The fire acts with equal force on every part of the still, and a greater heat may be applied to her, without burning. 2d. It has a great tendency to prevent the still house from smoking.

When the wall of the flue is completed round the still, and raised so high, that a brick when laid on the top of the wall will extend to the rivets in the breast of the still or upper rivets, then completely plaster very smooth and even, the inside of the

Kentucky's candy makers are no strangers to the blessed-by-heaven marriage of chocolate and bourbon. One of my favorites is Old Kentucky Chocolates' version of the bourbon truffle. (They actually make four (☺) types of bourbon confections!) Other area bourbon ball makers include, *but aren't limited to*, Ruth Hunt Candy and Rebecca Ruth Candy. There are no rules that say you must pick a favorite, but a good Kentuckian will insist on trying them all, preferably more than once. If you have a favorite place to buy bourbon chocolates, let me know!

flue, and then cover the flue with a layer of brick, with a slight fall, or leaning a little from the still outwards, so that if water

were dropped thereon, it would run off outwardly, carefully laying a layer of clay on the top of the wall, on which the brick may rest, and thereby prevent the brick from burning the still; carefully forming the brick with the trowel, so as to fit the wall and rest more safely—cautiously covering them well with clay, etc.. and closing every crevice or aperture, to prevent smoke from coming through or the heat from deserting the flue until it passes to the chimney from the flue; then fill the still with water, and put a flow fire under her to dry the work. When the wall begins to dry, lay on a coat of mortar, (such as the next receipt directs), about two inches thick, when this begins to dry, lay a white coat of lime and sand-mortar, smoothing well with a trowel; rubbing it constantly and pressing it severely with the trowel to prevent it from cracking.

There are many modes of setting stills and bringing the fire up by flues variously constructed, but I have found the foregoing plan to afford as great a saving of fuel, and bringing the still to a boil as early as any other.

HOW TO PREVENT THE PLASTERING ROUND STILLS FROM CRACKING

This method of making water proof plastering on stills, is done entirely in making the mortar, and putting it on, in making which, good clay and lime are absolutely necessary.

When the mortar for the first coat is thoroughly worked, put as much brock of rye straw into it, as can be worked in, so that when the coat is put on, it may have a greater appearance of straw than mortar, when dry, and covered with the second coat composed of lime mortar, well rubbed and pressed with the trowel until it be dry. A covering put on of those materials, will be found to continue firm and compact without cracking, as in the common mode.

THE BEST METHOD OF BOILING TWO, THREE OR MORE STILLS OR KETTLES WITH ONE FIRE OR FURNACE

This method has been found to answer in some instances, and may perhaps do generally if properly managed.

The tulip-shaped glasses are perfect for taking your bourbon drinking to the next level. Also referred to as nosing glasses, it's said that the shape helps carry bourbon's complex aromas to the nose.

I will here give the result of my own experiments.

I set a singling still holding 180 gallons on a furnace of 18 by 14 inches, and 4 feet six inches long, with the bottom to the fire, she had a common head and worm with scrapers and chains in her. I extended the flue, (or after passing it round her), to the doubling still which it likewise went round—but to prevent too much heat from passing to the doubling still, I fixed a shutter in the flue of the singling still, immediately above the intersection of the flue of the doubling still, to turn all the heat round her, and another shutter in the flue of the doubling still at the intersection of the flue of the singling still, to shut the heat off from the doubling still if necessary.

With this fixture I run six hogsheads off in every twenty-four hours and doubled the same, with the same heat and fire. I likewise had a boiler under which I kept another fire, which two fires consumed about three cords and a half of wood per week, distilling at the rate of sixty-five bushels of grain per week, and making about one hundred and ninety gallons in the same time.

Before I adopted this method I kept four fires going, and made about the same quantity of whiskey, consuming about four and a half cords of wood per week, and was obliged to have the assistance of an additional distiller per week. I have since heard of the adoption of this plan with more success than I experienced.

TO SET A DOUBLING STILL

As spirits can hardly be burned or singed in a doubling still, if not before done in singling, all the precaution necessary is to set them in the best method for saving fuel, and preserving the still.

The instructions given for setting a singling still, is presumed to be adequate to setting a doubling still.

> *"To a Kentuckian of exquisite Bluegrass essence, the drinking of bourbon is not a vice; sipping it with intentionality helps one define more clearly what a vice is."*
>
> —Steve Flairty
> Author of Kentucky's Everyday Heroes

HOW TO PREVENT THE SINGLING STILL FROM BURNING

If the singling still be well set, and is carefully greased with a piece of bacon, tallow or hard soap, every time she is filled, she will seldom burn, but if she does burn or singe notwithstanding these precautions, it will be advisable to take her down and set her up anew ten times, rather than have her burned.

Photo credit: Old Pogue Distillery

With a history that dates back to the Civil War, Old Pogue Distillery is located in Maysville, Kentucky, which was once part of Old Bourbon County, Virginia.

Bourbon Sweet Potato Pie
Submitted by Mary Sanders

My Aunt Mary (Auntie M) passed along this recipe from my grandmother, Tootsie Blankenship Wright. While such a dish is not that unusual, Mamaw Tootsie was a teetotaler as far as I knew. So her use of bourbon is a bit surprising, as is the fact that she apparently never let any bourbon go to waste.

"I remember the first time Mamaw made it with the added secret ingredient (bourbon)," Aunt Mary said. "We all had to guess what the secret ingredient was! She was so proud of her new culinary adventure!"

4 cups mashed sweet potatoes
I stick butter, melted
I tsp. vanilla
2 eggs (well beaten)
1/3 cup evaporated milk
3/4 tsp cinnamon
1/2 cup white sugar
1/3 to 1/2 cup bourbon

Topping:
2 cups brown sugar
I cup flour
I cup chopped pecans
2/3 cup melted butter

Combine first 8 ingredients in a large mixing bowl; beat with electric mixer on medium speed until smooth. Spoon mixture into a lightly greased 1 1/2-quart casserole. Mix together ingredients for topping, and sprinkle evenly over potato mixture.

Bake at 350° for 30 minutes or until thoroughly heated.

Chapter 7

HOW TO CLARIFY WHISKEY, ETC.

Take any vessel of convenient size, take one end out and make it clean, by scalding or otherwise; bore the bottom full of holes, a quarter of an inch in diameter—lay thereon three folds of flannel, over which spread ground maple charcoal and burnt brick-dust, made to the consistence of mortar, with whiskey, about two inches thick, pour your whiskey or brandy thereon, and let it filter through the charcoal, flannel, etc.. after which you will find the spirit to have scarcely any taste or smell of whiskey. Elevate the filtering cask so as to leave room to place a vessel to receive the spirit under it.

HOW TO MAKE A BRANDY RESEMBLING FRENCH BRANDY, FROM RYE WHISKEY OR APPLE BRANDY

Clarify the whiskey as the above receipt directs, after thus

Aren't these the cigar box and bourbon bottle lamps the coolest?! They're one example of how Mark and Camille Thomas are finding unique and practical ways to repurpose bourbon bottles, among other things, in their product line. From candles to pillows, barrel heads to bar stools, they're offering a great line-up of bourbon-themed products. They're on Facebook at Rustic Reinvented Lexington.

purifying, add one third or one fourth of French brandy, and it will be then found strongly to resemble the French brandy in taste and smell—and if kept a few years, will be found more salutary and healthful than French brandy alone. This mode of clarifying rids the spirit of any unpleasant flavour received in the process of distillation or from bad materials, and moreover, from all those vicious, poisonous properties contracted in the still or worm from copper; such as fetid oil from the malt, which frequently unites with the verdigris, and combines so effectually with whiskey, that it may possible require a frequent repetition of this mode of clarifying, to rid it completely of any unpleasant taste or property contracted as above stated.

HOW TO MAKE A SPIRIT RESEMBLE JAMAICA SPIRIT OUT OF RYE WHISKEY

This is done precisely in the manner laid down in the receipt for French brandy.

HOW TO MAKE A RESEMBLANCE OF HOLLAND GIN OUT OF RYE WHISKEY

Put clarified whiskey, with an equal quantity of water, into your doubling still, together with a sufficient quantity of juniper berries, prepared; take a pound of unflacked lime, immerse it in three pints of water, stir it well—then let it stand three hours, until the lime sinks to the bottom, then pour off the clear lime water, with which boil half an ounce of isinglass cut small, until the latter is dissolved—then pour it into your doubling still with a handful of hops, and a handful of common salt, put on the head and set her a running; when she begins to run, take the first half gallon (which is not so good), and reserve it for the next still you fill—as the first shot generally contains something that will give an unpleasant taste and color to the gin. When it looses proof at the worm, take the keg away that contains the gin, and bring it down to a proper strength with rain water, which must previously have been prepared, by having been evaporated and condensed in the doubling still and cooling tub.

This gin when fined, and two years old, will be equal, if not superior to Holland gin.

The isinglass, lime water and salt, helps to refine it in the still, and the juniper berries gives the flavor or taste of Holland gin.

About thirteen pounds of good berries, are sufficient for one barrel.

Be careful to let the gin as it runs from the worm, pass through a flannel cloth, which will prevent many unpleasant particles from passing into the liquor, which are contracted in the condensation, and the overjuice imbibed in its passage through the worm.

THE BEST METHOD OF MAKING COMMON COUNTRY GIN.

Take of singlings a sufficient quantity to fill the doubling still, put therein ten or twelve pounds of juniper berries, with one shovel full of ashes, and two ounces alum—put on the bead, and run her off, as is done in making whiskey. This is the common mode of making country gin; but is in this state little superior to whiskey, save as to smell and flavor.

It is therefore in my mind, that the mode of clarifying, prescribed, ought to be pursued in all distilleries, so far as

The Kentucky Bourbon Boys sent me this meme. Funny —yet oh-so-very-accurate.

necessary to make a sufficient quantity of good spirit for any market convenient—the supply of respectable neighbors, who may prefer giving a trifle more per gallon, than for common stuff and for domestic use. And moreover, I think the distiller will meet a

LORD,
GIVE ME COFFEE
TO CHANGE THE THINGS
I CAN CHANGE
& WHISKEY
TO ACCEPT THE ONES
I CAN NOT

generous price for such clarified, and pure spirit, as he may send to a large mercantile town for sale—as brewers and others, frequently desire such for mixing, brewing, making brandies in the French and Spanish mode, and spirits after the Jamaica custom. And after the establishment of a filtering tub or hopper, prepared as before described, with holes, flannel or woollen cloth, and plenty of maple charcoal, and burnt brick-dust, a distiller may always find leisure to attend to the filtration; indeed it will be found as simple and easy, as the process for making ley from ashes in the country for soap. But I would suggest that spirit prepared and clarified in this way, should be put into the sweetest and perfectly pure casks.

New barrels will most certainly impart color, and perhaps some taste, which would injure the sale, if intended for a commercial town market, and for brewing, or mixing with spirits, from which it is to receive its flavor.

For my own use, I would put this spirit into a nice sweet cask, and to each barrel I would add a pint of regularly, and well browned wheat, not burned but roasted as much as coffee.

The taste of peach brandy may be imparted to it by a quantity of peach stone kernels, dried, pounded and stirred into the cask; in this way, those who are fond of the peach brandy flavor, may drink it without becoming subject to the pernicious consequences that arise from the constant use of peach brandy. Peach brandy, unless cleansed of its gross and cloying properties, or is suffered to acquire some years of age, has a cloying effect on the stomach, which it vitiates, by destroying the effect of the salival and gastric juices, which have an effect on aliment, similar to that of yeast on bread, and by its singular properties prevents those juices from the performance of their usual functions in the fermentation of the food taken into the stomach—producing acid and acrimonious matter, which in warm climates generates fevers and agues. Apple brandy has not quite a similar but equally pernicious effect, which age generally removes—indeed, age renders it a very fine liquor, and when diluted with water, makes a very happy beverage, gives life and animation to the digesting powers, and rarely leaves the stomach heavy, languid and cloyed. Then both those, (indeed, all liquors,) ought to be avoided when new, by persons of delicate habit, and those who do not exercise freely. A severe exercise and rough life, generally enables the stomach to digest the most coarse food, by liquor, however new.

ON FINING LIQUORS

Isinglass is almost universally used in fining liquors. Take about half an ounce to the barrel—beat it fine with a hammer, lay it in a convenient vessel, pour thereon two gallons whiskey, or a like quantity of the liquor you are about to fine, let it soak two or three days, or until it becomes soft enough to mix—then stir it effectually, and add the white and shells of half a dozen

This wall of bourbon at Woodford Reserve Distillery is an eye-catching display of sophistication.

eggs—beat them up together and pour them into the cask that is to be fined, then stir it in the cask, bung it slightly, after standing three or four days it will be sufficiently fine, and may be drawn off into a clean cask.

ON COLORING LIQUORS

One pound of brown sugar burnt in a skillet almost to a cinder, add a quart of water, which when stirred, will dissolve the sugar—when dissolved, this quantity will color three barrels.

A pint of well parched wheat put into a barrel will color it, and give more the appearance of a naturally acquired color, and an aged taste or flavor.

TO CORRECT THE TASTE OF SINGED WHISKEY

Although this cannot be done effectually without clarifying, as prescribed, but Bohea tea will in a great measure correct a slight singe—a quarter of a pound may be tried to the barrel.

TO GIVE AN AGED FLAVOR TO WHISKEY

This process ought to be attended to by every distiller, and with all whiskey, and if carefully done, would raise the character, and add to the wholesomeness of domestic spirits.

It may be done by clarifying the singlings as it runs from the still—let the funnel be a little broader than usual, cover it with two or more layers of flannel, on which place a quantity of finely beaten maple charcoal, through which let the singlings filter into your usual receiving cask. When doubling, put some lime and charcoal in the still, and run the liquor through a flannel—when it loses proof at the worm, take away the cask, and bring it to proof with rain water that has been distilled. To each hogshead of whiskey, use a pound of Bohea tea, and set it in the sun for two weeks or more, then remove it to a cool cellar, and when cold it will have the taste and flavor of old whiskey. If this method was pursued by distillers and spirits made 2d and 3d proof, it would not only benefit the seller, but would be an advantage to the buyer and consumer—and was any particular distiller to pursue this mode and brand his casks, it would raise the character of his liquor, and give it such an ascendancy as to preclude the sale of any other, beyond what scarcity or a n emergency might impel in a commercial city.

If distillers could conveniently place their liquor in a high loft, and suffer it to fall to the cellar by a pipe, it would be greatly improved by the friction and ebullition occasioned in the descent and fall.

Lee, one of the tour guides at Buffalo Trace Distillery, pours a few shots and talks a little bourbon after taking a group of visitors on the hard hat tour on the distillery grounds. If you play your cards right, he'll even make you a root beer float—and trust me, it's so good it'll rival your mama's sweet tea.

Bourbon and Bacon Party Mix

Have you ever noticed how a conversation about bourbon can lead to instant friendships? It's true! It can also lead to bourbon recipes, like this one I learned about from a local crafter. She told me I simply must try a "to die for" party mix that featured both bourbon and (wait for it...) BACON! I can't make this stuff up! In the name of Southern Hospitality, I tracked down the recipe, knowing I had to share it with all y'all. Make it today. You'll love it!

1 15 oz. bag Chex Mix® traditional snack mix
1 cup pecan halves
½ lb bacon (6 to 8 slices), crisply cooked and crumbled
½ cup packed brown sugar
½ cup butter
¼ cup light corn syrup
2 tablespoons bourbon
¾ teaspoon chipotle chili powder

Heat oven to 300°F. Line two sheet pans with foil. Spray foil with cooking spray. In large bowl, mix snack mix, pecans and bacon. Set aside.

In 2-quart saucepan, heat brown sugar, butter and corn syrup over medium heat, stirring occasionally, until bubbly around edges. Cook 5 minutes, stirring occasionally; remove from heat. Cool 2 minutes. Carefully stir in bourbon and chipotle chili powder. Pour over snack mixture; toss until evenly coated.

Spread snack mixture on pans. Bake 15 minutes, stirring every 5 minutes, to caramelize mixture. Cool completely, about 1 hour. Break into pieces. Store covered in refrigerator.

Chapter 8

OBSERVATIONS ON WEATHER

Some seasons are better for fermentation than others. Should a hail storm occur in the summer, the distiller should guard against cooling off with water in which hail is dissolved, for it will not work well. If a thundergust happens when the hogsheads are in the highest state of fermentation, the working will nearly cease, and the stuff begin to contract an acidity. And when in the spring the frost is coming out of the ground, it is unfortunate when the distiller is obliged to use water impregnated with the fusions of the frost, such being very injurious to fermentation —Those changes and occurrences ought to be marked well, to enable a provision against their effects. This will be found difficult without the assistance of a barometer, to determine the changes

The Devil's Cut and the Angel's Share

We all know that the best things in life are worth the sacrifice required to attain them. Good bourbon is no exception—not everything that goes into the barrel makes it back out. The devil's cut is the liquid goodness trapped in the barrel, soaked up by thirsty barrel staves. (It's also the name of Jim Beam's Devil's Cut Straight Bourbon Whiskey.) The angel's share, on the other hand refers to the portion of liquid that evaporates during the aging process. The longer it ages, the less bourbon remains in the barrel. After a few years, the angel's share can really add up! But let's be honest. Who among us would fault the angels for taking their fair share?

of the weather—a thermometer, to ascertain correctly the heat of the atmosphere, and to enable a medium and temperature of the air to be kept up in the distillery; and from observation to acquire a knowledge of the degree of heat or warmth, in which the mashing in the hogsheads ferments to the greatest advantage, and when this is ascertained, a distiller may in a close house sufficiently ventilated, and provided with convenient windows, always keep up the degree or temperature in the air, most adapted to the promotion of fermentation, by opening his windows or doors to admit air, as a corrective; or by keeping them closed in proportion to the coldness of the weather:—And a hydrometer, useful in measuring and ascertaining the extent of water. Instructions for the management of those instruments generally attend them, it is therefore unnecessary for me to go into a detail on this subject. But it is absolutely necessary that the careful and scientific distiller should possess them, especially the two former, to guard against the changes of the weather, and preserve the atmosphere in the distillery, always equally warm.

OBSERVATIONS ON WATER

Distillers cannot be too particular in selecting good water for distilling, when about to erect distilleries.

Any water will do for the use of the condensing tubs or coolers, but there are many kinds of water that will not answer the purpose of mashing or fermenting to advantage; among which are snow and limestone water, either of which possess such properties, as to require one fifth more of grain to yield the same quantity of liquor, that would be produced while using river

Gimme Three Sips

When it comes to tasting bourbon, there are plenty of experts who know far more than I. So if you want to nail the nose and the finish, use the proper glass and pick the right bourbon to begin your journey, consult one of the experts. Meanwhile, here's a three-step sip version that works well for me.

- The **first** sip prepares the palette.
- The **second** sip gives you the general feel.
- The **third** sip gives you the flavor.

water.

Any water will answer the distillers purpose, that will dissolve soap, or will wash well with soap, or make a good lather for shaving.

River or creek water is the best for distilling except when mixed with snow or land water from clay or ploughed ground. If no river or creek water can be procured, that from a pond, supplied by a spring, if the bottom be not very muddy will do, as the exposure to the sun, will generally have corrected those properties inimical to fermentation. Very hard water drawn from a deep well, and thrown into a cistern, or reservoir and exposed to the sun and air for two or three days, has been used in mashing with success, with a small addition of chop grain or malt. I consider rain water as next in order to that from the river, for mashing and fermentation. Mountain, slate, gravel and running water, are all preferable to limestone, unless impregnated with minerals—many of which are utterly at variance with fermentation. With few exceptions, I have found limestone, and all spring water too hard for mashing, scalding or fermenting.

PRECAUTIONS AGAINST FIRE

Cannot be too closely attended to. The store house, or cellar for keeping whiskey in, ought to be some distance from the distillery, and the liquor deposited, and all work necessary in it done by day, to avoid all possible danger arising from candles or lamps, from which many serious calamities have occurred. Suppose the cellar or place of deposit to be entered at night by a person carrying a lamp or candle, and a leaking cask takes his attention, in correcting the leak, he may set his lamp on the ground covered with whiskey, or he may drop by chance one drop of burning oil on a small stream of whiskey, which will communicate like gun powder, and may cause an explosion, which may in all likelihood destroy the stock on hand, the house, and the life of the individual.—On this subject it is not necessary I should say much, as every individual employed about a distillery must have some knowledge of the value of life and property.

From Glencairn nosing glasses and wine glasses to highballs and lowballs, and of course the ever-popular red Solo cup, you'll find that glasses for drinking bourbon and promoting bourbon are as plentiful as the whiskey itself.

Bourbon and Bacon Brittle

I know. Here we go again with bourbon and bacon. You can thank me later. ☺

For the brittle:

3/4 cup sugar
1/2 cup light corn syrup
1/2 cup water
1 T unsalted butter
2 T bourbon
1 t vanilla
1 t. baking soda
1/2 cup chopped pecans
Pinch of red pepper
Sea salt

For the candied bacon:

12 strips thick-cut bacon
3 T bourbon
3 T brown sugar

Preheat oven to 400 degrees. Lay bacon strips on a foil-lined baking sheet. Brush each side with bourbon and sprinkle with brown sugar. Bake 13-15 minutes until bacon is crispy and begins to caramelize. Chop bacon into small pieces. Measure out all ingredients so they're ready to go.

Lightly toast pecans and a pinch of red pepper in skillet or oven. Line a baking sheet with parchment paper.

In medium sauce pan, combine sugar, corn syrup and water, stirring constantly over medium heat until sugar dissolves and mixture starts to boil. Increase heat and cook until candy thermometer reads 290 degrees. Remove from heat. Quickly stir in remaining ingredients (careful with the bourbon) and pour onto baking sheet. Work quickly and spread as think as possible. Sprinkle with sea salt if desired, then allow to cool at least 20 minutes. Break into pieces and store in an airtight container for up to a week.

Chapter 9

THE DUTY OF THE OWNER OF A DISTILLERY

The main and first object of the proprietor of a distillery, is gain or profit—and the second, it is natural, should be the acquiring a character or reputation for his liquor, and a desire to excel neighboring distilleries—in both of which, neglect and sloth will insure disappointment.

The active, cleanly, industrious and attentive proprietor uses the following means.

First. He provides his distillery with good sound grain, hogsheads, barrels, kegs, funnels, brooms, malt, hops, wood, etc.. of all of which he has in plenty, nicely handled, and in good order. He also provides a hydrometer, thermometer, and particularly a barometer, duly observing the instructions accompanying each, their utility and particular uses.

Secondly. He is careful that his distiller does his duty, of

For more than 62 years, Master Distiller Jimmy Russell has been a part of Kentucky's bourbon industry at Wild Turkey. He's the longest-tenured, active Master Distiller in the global spirits industry. Often referred to as the Buddha of Bourbon and the Master Distiller's Master Distiller, Jimmy's a celebrity of sorts. Spend a few minutes with him and you'll see he exemplifies the virtues of a true southern gentleman, one who's never met a stranger. So keep an eye out when you head to Wild Turkey Distillery and jump at the opportunity to meet the man who's as legendary as the bourbon he crafts.

which he can be assured only, by rising at four o'clock, winter and summer, to see if the distiller is up and at his business, and that everything is going well—and to prepare everything and article necessary—to attend and see the hogs fed, and that the potale or slop be cold when given, and that the cattle be slopped—that the stills are not burning, nor the casks leaking, etc.. etc.. He observes the barometer, points out any changes in the weather, and pays an unremitted attention, seeing that all things are in perfect order, and enforcing any changes he may deem necessary.

On the other hand, indolence begets indolence—The proprietor who sleeps until after sun rise, sets an example to his distiller and people, which is too often followed—the distillery becomes cold from the want of a regular fire being kept up in her—the hogsheads cease to work or ferment, of consequence, they will not turn out so much whiskey—and there is a general injury sustained. And it may often occur, that during one, two or three days in the week, the distiller may want grain, wood, malt, hops or some necessary—and perhaps all those things may be wanting during the same day ... and of course, the distiller stands idle. The cattle, hogs, etc.. suffer; and from this irregular mode of managing, I have known the proprietor to sink money, sink in reputation, and rarely ever to attribute the effect to the right cause.

SYSTEM AND METHOD

A well timed observance of system and method are necessary in all the various branches of business pursued, and without which none succeeds so well.

And whilst the industrious, attentive and cleanly proprietor, may with certainty, calculate on a handsome profit and certain advantages to result from this business. He who conducts carelessly, may as certainly reckon on sustaining a general loss.

THE DUTY OF A HIRED DISTILLER

Is to rise at four o'clock every morning. Wash and clean out the boiler, fill her up with clean water, put fire under her, and to clean, fill and put fire under the singling still—to collect and put in order for mashing, his hogsheads—and as soon as the water is warm enough in the boiler to begin mashing, which he ought to finish as early in the day as possible; for when the mashing is done, he will have time to scald and clean his vessels, to attend his doubling and singling still, to get in wood for next day, and to make his stock yeast, if new yeast is wanting. In short, the distiller ought to have his mashing finished by twelve o'clock every day, to see and have everything in the still house, under his eye at the same time; but he ought never to attempt doing more than one thing at once—a distiller ought never to be in a hurry, but always busy. I have always remarked that the bustling unsteady distiller attempts doing two or three things at once, and rarely ever has his business in the same state of forwardness with the steady methodical character.

Bourbon Barbeque Pulled Chicken
Submitted by Marsha Hunt

Here's another great bourbon recipe from Marsha. She really should open a catering business (subtle hint).

2 small bone-in, skin on chicken breasts
2 skin on, bone in chicken thighs
2 bay leaves
1 small carrot, coarsely chopped
1/2 orange, sliced
1 small onion, quartered
Salt

1 cup ketchup
2 T each: Dijon mustard, dark brown sugar, maple syrup, cider vinegar, Worcestershire sauce
1 T black pepper
2 large chopped garlic cloves
Juice of half an orange
2 shots bourbon

Combine chicken with bay leaves, onion, carrot, orange and salt into pot, cover with water and bring to a boil. Reduce heat and cook on a slow rolling boil for 30 minutes. Remove chicken to cool, strain broth and return to pot. Boil to reduce slightly.

Pull meat from bone and shred.

In a separate pot, combine all other ingredient to make sauce. Simmer on medium low, stirring occasionally for about 20 minutes. Add 1 cup of broth and shredded chicken to sauce mixture and stir well. Serve on sandwich buns of choice.

Chapter 10

PROFITS OF A COMMON DISTILLERY

Profits arising from a distillery with two common stills, one containing 110 gallons, and one containing 65 gallons that is well conducted for 10 months. The calculations predicated on a site, distant about 60 miles from market. Due regard is paid to the rising and falling markets in the following statement. The selling price of whiskey will always regulate the price of grain, the distiller's wages, the prices of malt, hops, hauling, etc.. is rather above than below par.

Distillery, Dr.

1077 bushels corn, at 50 cents per bushel

$538.50

533 bushels rye at 60 cents

$309.80

96 bushels malt, at 70 ditto $ 67.20

60 pounds hops at 25 cents per pound	*$15*
100 cords of wood, at 2 dollars	*$200*
Distiller's wages per year and boarding	
	$204.70
Hauling whiskey, at 4 cents/gallon	*$204.70*
50 poor hogs at $4 each	*$200*
Total	
$1739.90	

		Contra Cr.
Buy 5118 gallons whiskey at 59 cents/gal	*$2559*	
50 fat hogs at $7 each		*$ 350*
		$ 2939
Leaving a balance of		*$1143.10*

I have charged nothing for hauling of grain, etc.. as the feed or slop for milk cows, young cattle, and fatting cattle, will more than pay that expense.

An estimate of the profits arising from a patent distillery, (col. Anderson's patent improved) 1 still of 110 with a patent head, 1 still of 85 gallons for a doubling still, and a boiler of metal, holding 110 gallons.

Distillery, Dr.		
To 2454 bushels corn, at 50 cents/bushel		*$1227*
1216 do. rye, at 60 cents do.		
		$729.60
200 do. malt at 70 cents do.	*$140*	
3870		

120 pounds hops, at 25 cents per lb	*$ 30*
100 cords wood, at $2 per cord	*$200*
2 distillers wages, boarding, &c.	*$400*
hauling whiskey, per gal at 4 cents	*$464.40*
120 poor hogs at $4 each	*$480*
Total Expense	*$3671*

11610 gal. of whiskey, 50 cents/gal	*$5805.50*
120 fat hogs at $7 each	*$ 840*
	$6645.50

Clear profit	*$2974.50*

Profit of a common distillery	*$1148.10*
Balance in favor of a patent distillery	*$1826.40*

To do the business of a patent distillery or to carry her on to advantage, requires a little more capital to start with—but

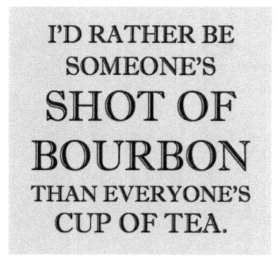

either the patent or common distillery, when they have run two or three months, managed by an attentive and brisk dealing man, will maintain, or keep themselves going.

Where wood is scarce and money plenty, the

patent distillery is certainly to be recommended, indeed, in all cases, I would recommend it, where the proprietor has money enough. It is by far the most profitable, and will sooner or later become in general use in this country.

OF HOGS

Raising, feeding and fattening hogs on potale, a business pursued and highly spoken of, but from my experience I have discovered that few good pigs can be raised entirely on potale—as it has a tendency to gripe and scour too much; but after they are weaned and a little used with slop, they will thrive well.

If a hog in a cold morning comes running to a trough full of slop, that is almost boiling, and is very hungry—their nature is so gluttonous & voracious, that it will take several mouthfuls before it feels the effects of the heat, and endangers the scalding of the mouth, throat and entrails—and which may be followed by mortification and death;—moreover, hot feeding is the cause of so many deaths, and ill-looking unhealthy pigs, about some distilleries—which inconvenience might be avoided by taking care to feed or fill the troughs before the boiling slop is let out from the still.

A distiller cannot be too careful of his hogs—as with care, they will be found the most productive stock he can raise—and without care unproductive.

The offals of distilleries and mills cannot be more advantageously appropriated than in raising of hogs—they are prolific, arrive at maturity in a short period, always in demand. Pork generally sells for more than beef, and the lard commands a higher price than tallow; of the value of pork and every part of this animal, it is unnecessary for me to enter into detail; of their great value and utility, almost every person is well acquainted.

The hog pens and troughs ought to be kept clean and in

good order, the still slop salted two or three times a week; when fattening, hogs should be kept in a close pen, and in the summer a place provided to wallow in water.

Hogs that are fed on potale, ought not to lie out at night, as dew, rain and snow injures them—indeed such is their aversion to bad weather, that when it comes on, or only a heavy shower of rain, away they run, full speed, each endeavoring to be foremost, all continually crying out, until they reach their stye or place of shelter.

At the age of nine months, this animal copulates first, and frequently earlier, but it is better engendering should be

What was once the Old Taylor Distillery, which opened in 1887, is now the location of Castle & Key Distillery. At the helm of operations is Marianne Barnes, who owns the distinction of being Kentucky's first female master distiller since Prohibition. Located on McCracken Road, Castle & Key will eventually include a restaurant and hotel.

prevented, until the age of eighteen months—for at an earlier age, the litter is uniformly small, and weakly, and frequently do not survive, besides the growth is injured. It is therefore better not to turn a sow to breeding, until from 18 to 24 months old.

The sow goes four months with pig, and yields her litter at the commencement of the fifth; soon after encourages and receives the boar, and thus produces two litters in the year. I have known an instance of three litters having been produced in the year from one female.

A sow ought not to be permitted to suckle her pigs more than two or three weeks, after which eight or nine only should be left with her, the rest sold, or sent to market, or killed for use—at the age of three weeks they are fit for eating, if the sow is well fed. A few sows will serve, and those kept for breeding, well selected from the litter, the residue, cut and splayed. Care and pains is due in the choice of the breed of hogs—the breeder had then better procure good ones, and of a good race at once, though the expense and trouble may seem material in the outset, yet the keeping will be the same, and the produce perhaps fifty per cent more.

After the pigs are weaned, they ought to be fed for the first two weeks on milk, water and bran, after which potale may be used in the room of milk. I would recommend a little mixed potale from an early period, and increase it, so as to render them accustomed to the slop gradually.

OF THE DISEASES OF HOGS

The only disease that I know of which seems to be peculiar to hogs, is a kind of leprosy, commonly called measles, when it seizes them, they become dull and sleepy, if the tongue is pulled out, the palate and throat will be found full of blackish spots, which appear also on the head, neck, and on the whole body—

the creature is scarce able to stand, and the roots of its bristles are bloody. As this disorder proceeds chiefly from their gluttony and filth, and hot drinking of potale and slop; to remedy which, it would be commendable to feed on cold potale, or scarcely milk warm, to keep them clean, to mix salt occasionally with the potale—tar their trough once a month, and give them a little ground antimony.

In fattening hogs I have known them improve rapidly, after eating the warm ashes from a fresh burned brush heap. Hickory or willow ashes will have an effect to destroy worms, and I think ought to be used, they will eat it dry, when put in their troughs.

ON FEEDING CATTLE AND MILCH COWS

Potale is a great creator of milk, and will increase the quantity greatly in cows yielding milk, but no so good. Young cattle thrive very well, that get hay or straw during the night. To fatten cattle there ought to be mixed with the slop, a little oil meal, or chopped flaxseed, or chopped corn. The cattle kept on still slop ought to get plenty of salt. Warm potale injures their teeth.

> *"Happiness is having a rare steak, a bottle of whiskey, and a dog to eat the rare steak.*
>
> —Johnny Carson

Bourbon-Sea Salt Caramels

There are a host of recipes for this delectable treat out there, but I'm partial to this one from the fine folks at bon appetit. *I think you will be, too!*

Nonstick vegetable oil spray
2 cups sugar
1/2 cup light corn syrup
1 14-oz. can sweetened condensed milk
1 stick unsalted butter, cut into small pieces
2 tablespoons Bourbon
1/2 teaspoon kosher salt
Flaky sea salt

Lightly coat an 8x8" baking pan with nonstick spray and line with parchment paper, leaving a 2" overhang on 2 sides; spray parchment.

Bring sugar, corn syrup, and ¼ cup water to a boil in a medium saucepan over medium-high heat until sugar is dissolved. Cook, swirling pan occasionally, until mixture turns a deep amber color, 8–10 minutes.

Remove pan from heat and whisk in sweetened condensed milk and butter (mixture will bubble vigorously) until smooth. Fit pan with thermometer and return to medium-low heat. Cook, whisking constantly, until thermometer registers 240°.

Remove from heat and whisk in bourbon and kosher salt. Pour into prepared pan; let cool. Sprinkle caramel with sea salt, cut into ¾" pieces, and wrap individually in parchment paper.

Caramels can be made 2 weeks ahead. Store wrapped tightly in plastic in airtight container at room temperature.

Chapter 11

OBSERVATIONS ON ERECTING DISTILLERIES

Those who are about to erect distilleries, have a handsome subject for consideration; the advantages, and the probable disadvantages that may arise from building on a particular site, or seat. The contiguity to a chopping mill is a material consideration—Wood forming an important article, should be taken into view—Grain merits also a great share of attention. The water which forms, by no means, the least important ingredient should be well analyzed; and a share of thought is due to the subject of a market for the whiskey, spirits and pork, produced from the establishment.—And should the water then prove good, soft and proper for fermentation, can be bro't over head, and the chopping mill is not very inconvenient, and wood convenient and cheap, and grain plenty and at reasonable prices, and a market within one hundred miles, I have little doubt but that with proper economy and observance of system, the establishment will prove very productive; and may be progressed in with cheerfulness, and a reasonable hope of a fair retribution to the owner.

A proper seat being fixed on, with sufficient fall to bring the water over head, for it is very material, and an immense saving of labor—material, because it prevents a loss, in running the stills, from pumping

Photo courtesy of Jeptha Creed Distillery

One of the latest additions to Kentucky Distilleries is Jeptha Creed in Shelby County. It is that county's first distillery since Prohibition. Visit jepthacreed.com for more information.

or want of water in the cooling tubs. The size of the house follows, as requiring some more than usual calculation—houses are generally made too small, giving great inconvenience, and preventing that nice attention to cleanliness, which forms a very important item in the process of distilling. I would recommend a size sufficiently large for three stills, and to mash six hogsheads per day—one of col. Anderson's patent improved stills, I would consider, in many situations, as most desirable; at all events, I would recommend the preparation of room enough for three stills, if even it should be the intention of the owner to erect but two—for it is very probable, that after some experience, he may determine to pursue the business more extensively, and add the patent still.

The size then established, I would recommend the lower story to be 10 feet high, this will leave room for the heated, or rarefied air to ascend in the summer above the cooler, and more necessary air in the warm season of the year, and prevent the unpleasant effect of a too warm air on the mashing hogsheads, and the sowing of the stuff in fermentation—and moreover, prevent the unpleasant effects of smoke on the distillers eyes. But it is important that the house should be erected on level ground with doors opposite each other, with plenty of windows to afford a draft and recourse of air, at pleasure, during the warm season; and so that in the winter it may be closed and preserved perfectly warm—to which end it is most expedient the lower story should be well built with stone and lime, and neatly plastered—the windows well glazed, with shutters etc.. Thus provided, and a thermometer placed in the center of the house, a proper temperature may be kept up in the air of the house—

According to the Kentucky Distillers Association: nearly 60 percent of every bottle of spirits in Kentucky goes to taxes or fees, with seven different taxes on Bourbon – including an ad valorem tax on barrels each and every year it ages. Distilleries paid $15.2 million in barrel taxes in 2013, up 52 percent since 2006.

image courtesy of 401Kcalculator.org

for there is a certain degree of warmth which exceeds for fermentation—this degree of heat, then correctly ascertained by the distiller, he may by a close attention to his duties, fires and the thermometer, always keep the air of the house in nearly that same and most approved state; and even by a well-timed observation guard against storms and casualties. To effectuate this grand and important object, some have divided the stills, placing the boiler at one end, and a singling and doubling still at the other; this mode will ensure, in cold weather, the success of the measure more fully—others have placed all the stills in the center of the building—a plan that will do better in the winter than in the summer, and one I think less favourably of than that of dividing them.

During the winter, the north or northwest side of the house should be kept quite close, permitting the house to be lighted from the more temperate southward exposure. To calculate the window sashes to open by hinges, or to be taken entirely out in the summer, at pleasure, is in my mind advisable.

Photo courtesy of Dane Schlea

The morning mist begins to lift on a cool fall morning at Glenns Creek Distillery.

Bourbon-Drenched Cherries

When the recipe requires little more than a mix and pour, you know you're onto something special! This recipe for drunk cherries couldn't be easier. Warning: they're kinda like that famous potato chip. You can't stop at just one. And yes, I speak from experience.

1 package dried cherries
1 cup Bourbon
1/4 to 1/2 cup honey or brown sugar
Pinch of nutmeg

Place cherries in a small lidded jar. In a small sauce pan, mix together bourbon, sugar and nutmeg over medium heat and stir until sugar is dissolved. Pour over cherries. Top the jar and allow cherries to soak up all that bourbon goodness for at least 12 hours.

Add them to mixed drinks, top off a favorite dessert or eat them straight out of the jar. Southern hospitality would dictate that these cherries would make a fine hostess gift. Or weekend brunch. ☺

Chapter 12

ON WINES

Presuming this work may be rendered more desirable to farmers, from the introduction of some receipts for making domestic wine from the common hedge grapes, or such as are common on fence rows and on high rich grounds, and which are pleasantly flavored after receiving frost, and also for making cider in the best mode for preservation. I have extracted a few from various author's.

RECEIPT FOR MAKING DOMESTIC WINE FROM THE AUTUMN BLUE GRAPE.

About the latter end of September or about the first white frosts, gather the grapes which with us grow along old fences and hedges—pick all the grapes from the stems that are juicy, allowing two bushels thus picked a little heaped, to the barrel. Mash them well between your hands in small parcels, either in earthen pans, or some convenient small vessels—put them when mashed into a tub together, and add a little water so as to soak the pumice....

After stirring them well together, squeeze the pumice out from the liquor with your hands, as clean as you can—then strain the juice through a hair sieve. If the juice seems not all extracted from the

Each September, visitors from Kentucky and around the world head to Bardstown for this six-day lineup of everything bourbon. From black-tie affairs and bourbon samplers to craft booths and concerts, the Bardstown festival offers a week of unmatched bourbon celebrations. For more information about the annual festival, visit kybourbonfestival.com

pumice at one soaking and squeezing, put water to the pumice and squeeze them over again; take care not to add too much water, lest there should be more than the cask will hold. If after all the ingredients are added, the cask is not full, it may then be filled up with water. To the liquor thus prepared, add two pounds of good, clean, rich low priced brown sugar, per gallon, stirring it in the tub until all the sugar be dissolved; let it remain in the tub, and in a day or two it will ferment, and the scum rise to the top, which must be carefully skimmed off—then put the wine into a clean nice barrel—do not bung it up tight. There is generally a fermentation in it the spring following, when the grape vines are in blossom, but racking it off just before that season will prevent its working too much. If it is wanted to be soon ripe for use, put a quart of good old brandy after it is racked off, to the barrel, and give it air by leaving the bung quite loose.

This mode of manufacturing wine for domestic use, is convenient and not expensive to those who have it in their power to manufacture maple sugar. But the nice housewife or husbandmen of ingenuity, will, I fancy, devise some more neat mode of compressing the juice from the grape—as pressing it by the hand, would seem less cleanly, though the fermentation generally cleanses sufficiently.

CURRANT WINE

Is managed in the same way. The same quantity of sugar is presumed to answer—The juice is generally well strained through cloths, and when well stirred, etc., with the sugar, and neatly racked off, is put by in a loft to ripen, in sweet casks.

DIRECTIONS FOR MAKING CIDER, BRITISH MODE.

The apples after being thrown into a heap should always be covered from the weather. The later the cider is made the better, as the juice is then more perfectly ripened, and less danger to be feared from fermentation. Nothing does more harm to cider than a mixture of rotten apples with the sound. The apples ought to be ground so close as to break the seeds which gives the liquor an agreeable bitter. The pumice should be pressed through hair bags, and the juice strained through two sieves, the uppermost of hair, the lower of muslin. After this the cider should be put into open casks, when great attention is necessary to discover the exact time in which the pumice still remaining in the juice, rises on the top, which happens from the third to the tenth day, according as the weather is more or less warm. This body does not remain on top more than two hours; consequently, care should be taken to draw off the cider before it sinks, which may be done by means of a plug. When drawn off, the cider is put into casks. Particular attention is again required to prevent the fermentation, when the least inclination towards it is discovered. This may be done by a small quantity of cider spirits, about one gallon to the hogshead. In March the cider should be again drawn off, when all risque of fermentation ceases. Then it should be put into good sweet casks, and in three years from that time, it will be fit for bottling. Old wine casks are to be preferred; those which contain rum are ruinous to cider. Large earthen vessels might be made with or without glazing, which would be preferable to any wooden vessel whatever. When we compare this with the hasty American mode of making cider, it is not to be wondered at that the English cider so infinitely excels ours.

THE FOLLOWING IS A VERY HIGHLY APPROVED AMERICAN MODE OF MAKING CIDER

Take care to have every necessary utensil to be made use of in the whole process, perfectly clean and free from every

The Bourbon Classic, held each year in Louisville, explores the best of the best in the bourbon world. For information on this event, visit bourbonclassic.com.

foreign smell. For this purpose, before you begin your work, let your mill, trough and press be made perfectly clean, by thoroughly washing, and if necessary, with scalding water. The casks are another material object, and if musty, or any other bad smell, one end should be taken out, and with shavings burn the inside; then scrub them clean, and put in the head, scald them well afterwards, and drain them perfectly; when dry, bung them tight and keep them in a cool shady place until wanted for use. The apples should be quite ripe, and all the unripe and rotten ones, leaves, and every other thing that can tend to give the cider any disagreeable taste, carefully separated from them. I have found from careful attention and many experiments, that it is a great advantage to the cider to be separated from the gross parts as soon as possible; for this purpose, I tried several methods: that which I found succeeded the best, I shall now relate, as by following it, I was able to preserve my cider in a sound state, though made in the early part of the season.

I took a large pipe, of about 150 gallons, had one of the heads taken out, and on the inside of the other laid on edge, four strips of boards, two inches wide, and on these strips placed a false bottom, filled with gimlet holes, three inches apart. On this false bottom, I put a hair cloth, (old blanket or swingline tow will do) so as to prevent any sand from washing into the space between the true and false bottoms; I procured a quantity of coarse sand, which was carefully washed in repeated waters, until it would not discolor the clean water—then dried the sand, put it in the pipe, on the hair cloth, (coarse blanket or swingline tow,) about 9 inches thick.

Thus having everything in readiness, I went through the process of making, as quick as possible, by having the apples ground fine early in the morning, putting them in the press as fast as they were ground; and then in sufficient quantities pressed out the juice, and put it over the sand in the cask, (having previously bored a gimlet hole in the side of the cask), between the true and false bottoms, in which I introduced a large goose-quill, stopped with another. The pipe was placed so high, as to admit of a cask under it, to receive the liquor as it ran from the quill, which, if rightly managed, will be perfectly fine, and being put away in a cool cellar, and stopped close, will keep well, and prove of an excellent quality.

This process is easy, and in every person's power to execute, as the liquor, by being cleared, from its gross feculences, will not run into that violent fermentation, so destructive to the fine vinous flavor, which renders good cider so pleasing a drink.

Query.

Would not a quart of good apple brandy to each barrel of cider, made in this way, prevent any fermentation?

But it is generally believed that cider is the better for having undergone a fermentation,

Margaret Hancock, left, Pam Switzer and Mark Neikirk were part of the 2016 Bourbon Chase, a 200-mile relay race along the bourbon trail that takes runners through the beautiful Bluegrass State. Want to run? Visit bourbonchase.com.

becoming then more active and light; cider that has undergone condensation, or has been boiled down until strong, has been found to keep sound some length of time, but it is too heavy and destructive to the appetite, cloying the digesting powers.—And by too frequent use, I fancy, will ultimately produce ague and fevers; and I fear, cider made according to the foregoing receipt, would have a similar effect, but in a lesser degree.

I would recommend after a due attention to cleanliness, in the apple mill, trough, press and casks, that the apples be assorted, and having been exposed to the air, under a roof or shed some time, selecting the sound only, that they be ground fine, and let stand soaking in the pumice twelve hours, and then pressed off, through a clean rye straw cheese (being the most common and convenient in the country,) and when flowing from the press, a vessel should be provided, with the bottom full of gimlet holes, in the style of a riddle, on which lay a coarse cloth, then a layer of clean sand, over which a parcel of coarse rye straw, and suffer it to filter through this vessel into the large receiving tub; the rye straw will intercept the coarser pieces of pumice, and may be changed frequently—This mode will rid the liquor of all the coarser pieces of pumice—then I would recommend that the cider should be placed in open hogsheads, such as are used for mashing grain in distilleries; those being raised about two feet and an half high on logs or a scaffolding, under a shade or covering—a spile hole bored near the bottom of each, so as to admit a barrel to stand under the spile—in this state, I would recommend it to stand until it undergoes a fermentation, carefully watching the top, and when the pumice is found to have risen, to skim it off carefully, then having previously provided sweet barrels, draw it off by the spile hole, adding from a pint to a quart of apple brandy to each barrel of strong cider, bung it up tight, and store it where the frost will not injure it. In this way, I presume it will keep well—and if the party be so disposed, I would recommend any bottling to be done in April, and during clear weather, though it is safe to bottle immediately after having undergone a thorough fermentation.

THE FOLLOWING RECEIPT TO MAKE AN EXCELLENT AMERICAN WINE...

...was communicated to the Burlington Society for promoting domestic manufactures, by Joseph Cooper, Esq. of Gloucester county, state of New Jersey, and ordered to be published—which, from its extreme simplicity, and economy, shewing the convenience with which a very pleasant, healthful beverage, may be kept by every family in our country, is published in this work. And moreover, as it may have, in some degree, the happy effects of correcting the baneful and pernicious effects of coffee, which is so commonly used for breakfast in our state at present.

Coffee, when first introduced, was used as a medicine only, and given only in a well clarified state, and sparingly—both from its soothing and pleasant effect, it become common, and now it is almost the only beverage used at breakfast by the farmers of Pennsylvania, and indeed, people suppose the morning repast is not genteel, unless the board is decorated with this foreign

The Kentucky Bourbon Hall of Fame was created in 2001 and is the highest honor given in the bourbon industry. Induction ceremonies take place each fall during the Kentucky Bourbon Festival.

beverage. If it was used in a moderately strong well clarified state, it would be less injurious, but it is too frequently set down in a nondescript state, difficult to be named, mixed with the grounds, and so far from clear, as to b0e entitled to the epithet of muddy, and sweetened with bad sugar, carrying with it to the simply ignorant family, using it in this state, the cause in a great measure of destroying the tone of the stomach, overloading it, and by and by, the introduction of a kind of dumb ague, or chill, followed with a fever, and often creating intermitting and remitting fevers—consequences arising out of the free use of bad provisions—which diseases are oftentimes kept up by the use of this infamously prepared coffee, for when the country people get sick, coffee is too frequently used as the only diet.

It is particularly injurious to bilious habits—souring on the stomach, becoming acid, creating acidity, and preventing the glandular juicy supplies from producing the usual fermentation of the food in the stomach—rendering the chyle vitiated, which in its usual route, imparts from the intestines, nourishment to the blood. Thus conveying its baneful properties by this active vehicle, chyle to the blood, rendering it fetid, discolored and by and by, often as difficult to be named in its adulterated state as the composition which gave rise to it. Had we not very many instances of new diseases—complaints which the most eminent of the medical faculty can with difficulty name, or treat with judgment, without first having made many essays and experiments fatal to the lives of hundreds, which are increasing with every approaching season, and all since the adoption of coffee. (True, the free use of ardent spirits and other luxuries operating on the effects of indolence—of habits, produced by the wealth and independence of our agricultural and commercial people, and growing out of an imitation of the elevated, affluent of society, born to fortune, and the successful professional characters;) a doubt might present itself as to the propriety of attributing many of those new complaints to coffee ... but to a too plentiful use of bad provisions, and an indulgence of bad habits, we must attribute to them. And as badly made coffee is among the most pernicious kinds of food, and particularly when taken in the morning on an empty stomach, and that too made from very green coffee, (dreadfully poisonous when used too frequently before it acquires age and a whiter color,) it may be condemned with greater propriety. And whilst this beverage is condemned and so highly to be disapproved of, it is well if we can invent a light, pure, active and healthful beverage to be taken freely, between or at meals, calculated in its nature to correct in some degree, the unhappy effects of bad provisions—it is therefore I mention the…

RECEIPT FOR MAKING HONEY WINE

I put a quantity of the comb from which the honey had been drained, into a tub, to which I add a barrel of cider,

WILD TURKEY

OLD TIME COAL MINER

My dad passed along these two decanters—one from Wild Turkey and the other a product of the Commonwealth Distillery. Although the age of the turkey is unknown, the miner bears a date of 1976. From what I can gather, it's probably not a good idea to drink the contents because of lead issues. As for these decanters, though, the liquor was consumed many years ago. ☺

immediately from the press; this mixture was well stirred, and left to soak for one night. It was then strained before a fermentation took place, and honey was added until the weight of the liquor was sufficient to bear an egg. It was then put into a barrel, and after the fermentation commenced, the cask was filled every day for three or four days, with water, that the filth might work out of the bung hole. When the fermentation moderated, I put the bung in loosely, lest stopping it tight, might cause the cask to burst. At the end of five or six weeks the liquor

Logo credit: Kentucky Bourbon Trail

The Kentucky Bourbon Trail began in 1999 as a way to promote and pay homage the art, science, history and tradition of Kentucky bourbon. The trail currently features nine distilleries across the Bluegrass. For more information, visit kybourbontrail.com.

was drawn off into a tub, and the white of eight eggs well beaten up, with a pint of clean sand, were put into it—I then added a gallon of cider spirit, and after mixing the whole well together, I returned it into the cask, which was well cleaned, bunged it tight and placed it in a proper situation for racking it off when fine. In the month of April following, I drew it off for use, and found it equal in my opinion, to almost any foreign wine—in the opinion of many good judges it was superior.

This success has induced me to repeat the experiments for three years, and I am persuaded that by using the clean honey, instead of the comb, as above described; such an improvement might be made as would enable the citizens of the United States, to supply themselves with a truly federal and wholesome wine, which would not cost more than twenty cents per gallon, were all the ingredients procured at the market prices, and would have the peculiar advantage over all other wines, hitherto attempted in this country, that it contains no foreign mixture whatever, but is made from ingredients produced on our own farms.

Doubtless the foregoing wine will be found strong, and if not well clarified, or rather fined, may be heavy—and therefore will be found excellent when diluted freely with water, and when about to be drank, two thirds of water will be found necessary, and an improvement.

Bottling the foregoing wine in April, will certainly render it more excellent, and I fancy it ought to be drank mixed with water, during warm weather, and between meals, as in its pure state it may be found heavy. The gentleman who made the foregoing experiments, drew it off in kegs—this we presume was done to prevent its souring—as cider will suffer, and become hard after broaching the cask, whereas whilst full it remained sound. All American vinous liquors are liable to sour, because we rarely understand or practice the proper mode of manufacturing.

Complete cleansing and fermentation is absolutely necessary—and when fermented, it must be well fined, and then drawn off in nice casks, or bottled—bottling is certainly the most effectual, and if a farmer procures as many as three dozen of black bottles, they with three kegs of seven and a half gallons each, will hold the barrel. The kegs well bunged, will preserve the wine sound, and when a keg is broached, it must be immediately drawn off and bottled. The bottles when emptied, ought to be rinsed and stood up in an airy closet to drain.

TO MAKE ELDERBERRY WINE
The editor is happy in introducing the following receipts which he is confident is hardly known in America. The great quantities of the

Elderberry, which yearly goes to waste, might with very little trouble be manufactured into one of the most wholesome and agreeable wines ever introduced into America:

To every two quarts of berries, add one gallon of water, boil it half an hour, then strain it, and add to every gallon of liquor, two and a half pounds of sugar, then boil it together for half an hour, and skim it well; when cool (not cold) put in a piece of toasted bread, spread thick with brewer's yeast, to ferment. When you put this liquor into the barrel, which must be done the next day, add to every gallon of liquor, one pound of raisins, chopped, and stir all together in the barrel, once every day, for a week, then stop it close. It will not be fit to tap 'till the spring following the making; and the older the better.

REAL WOMEN DRINK BOURBON

If you think bourbon is a man's drink, think again. The bourbon culture has plenty of women who are connoisseurs of the distilled spirit. Among their offerings, the Bourbon Belle Society (bourbonbellesociety.com) and Bourbon Women Association (bourbonwomen.org) provide the fairer sex with bourbon education, networking and tasting events. These ladies will help you forgo a cocktail in favor of ordering your bourbon neat!

TO MAKE ELDERBERRY WINE, TO DRINK, MADE WARM, AS A CORDIAL

Equal quantities of berries and water boiled together, until the berries break, then strain off the liquor, and to every gallon thereof, put three pounds of sugar, and spice, to your palate, boil all up together, let it stand until it becomes cool, (not cold); then put in a piece of toasted bread, spread thick with brewer's yeast, to ferment, and in two or three days, it will be fit to put in the barrel, then stop it close. This will be fit to drink at Christmas, but the older the better.

From Kentucky Distillers' Association: Bourbon is a $3 billion industry here in Kentucky, generating 15,400 jobs with an annual payroll of $707 million. Spirits production and consumption pour more than $166 million in state and local tax coffers every year. For more information, visit kybourbon.com

Photo courtesy of Liz Wright

Mint Julip
Submitted by Betty Wright

As most people know, Derby Day is almost sacred in the Bluegrass State. The famous Mint Julip cocktail is synonymous with the Derby. Out on the track (or anywhere else for that matter) I believe my mother's Mint Julip recipe would come in several lengths ahead of any other.

For the syrup:

2 1/2 cups water
2 cups sugar
Juice of 2 oranges
Rind of one orange
Juice of 6 lemons
Rind of 2 lemons
2 large handfuls crushed mint leaves

Dissolve sugar in water and boil 10 minutes. Pour over juices and rinds while hot. Allow to sit at least one hour (more is better!). Strain. Store in refrigerator until ready to serve. If you have any leftovers, the syrup can be frozen. (Who are we kidding with the whole "leftovers" remark?!?)

To Serve:

Fill glass 2/3 full with crushed ice, add 5-6 T. syrup and a healthy shot of bourbon and top with ginger ale.

Chapter 13

TO MAKE RYE MALT FOR STILLING

Steep it twenty-four hours in warm weather, in cold, forty-eight, so in proportion as the weather is hot or cold; drain off the water, lay it in your malt cellar, about fifteen inches thick, for twelve hours; then spread it out half that thickness, sprinkling water on it at the same time; after that, it is to be turned three times a day with care, sprinkling water on as before. The thickness of the bed in this stage, must depend on the weather; work it in this way until the sprout is half as long as the grain, then throw it on your withering floor, wither it there for forty-eight hours; then put it on your kiln to dry.

OF BREWING BEER

As the following is intended principally for the use of private families, it will be necessary to begin with directions how to choose good Malt; for which, see Chapter 4.

OF THE BREWING VESSELS

To a copper that holds 36 gallons, the mash-tub ought to be at least big enough to contain six bushels of malt, and the copper of liquor, and room for mashing or stirring it: The under back, coolers and working tubs, may be rather fitted for the conveniency of the room, than to a particular size; for if one vessel be not sufficient to hold your liquor, you may take a second.

OF CLEANING AND SWEETENING CASKS & BREWING VESSELS

If a cask, after the beer is drank out, be well-stopped to keep out the air, and the lees remaining in it until you want to use it again, you will need only to scald it well, and take care of the hoops before you fill it; but if air gets into a foul empty cask, it will contract an ill scent in spite of scalding. A handful of bruised pepper boiled in the water you scald with, will take out a little musty smell; but the surest way is to take out the head of the cask, and let the cooper shave and burn it a little, and then scald it for use; if you cannot conveniently have a cooper to the cask, get some stone lime, and put about three pound into a barrel, (and proportionally to smaller or bigger vessels) and put to it about six gallons of cold water, bung it up, and shake it about for some time, and afterwards scald it well; or for want of lime, take a linen rag, and dip it in melted brimstone, and fasten one end to the bung, and light the other, and let it hang on the cask. You must give it a little air, else it will not burn; but keep in as much of the sulphur as you can. Scald it afterwards, and you will find no ill smell.

If you have new casks, before you fill them, dig places in

the earth, and lay them half their depth with their bung holes downward, for a week; and after well scalding them, you may venture to fill them.

Another way to proceed, if your brewing vessels are tinged with any ill smell, is to take unflacked lime and water, and with an old broom scrub the vessel whilst the water is hissing, with the lime; and afterwards take all this lime and water away, and put fresh water into the vessel, and throw some bay or common salt into each, and let it stand a day or two; and when you come to brew, scald your vessels, throw into them a little malt-dust or bran; and this will not only finish their sweetening, but stop them from leaking.

But since there is so much trouble in getting vessels sweet after they have been neglected, you ought to make all thorough clean after brewing, and once a month to fill your vessels with fair water, and let it off again in two or three days.

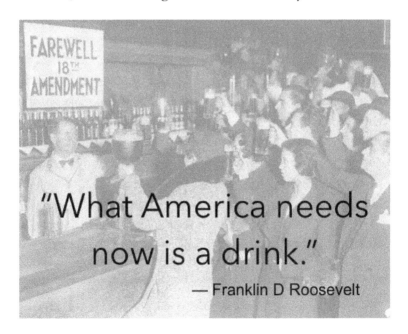

OF MASHING OR RAKING YOUR LIQUORS

Suppose you take six bushels of malt, and two pounds of hops, and would make of it one barrel of strong, and two barrels of small beer.

Heat your first copper of liquor for mashing, and strew over it a double handful of bran or malt; by which you will see when it begins to boil; for it will break and curl, and then it is fit to be let off into the mash tub, where it must remain until the steam is quite spent, and you can see your face in it, before you put in your malt; and then you begin to mash, stirring it all the while you are putting in the malt: but keep out about half a bushel dry, which you are to strew over the rest, when you have done stirring it, which will be as soon as you have well mixed it with the liquor, and prevented it from clodding.

After the dry malt is laid on, cover your mash tub with cloths, to prevent losing any spirit of the malt, and let it so remain for two hours. Meanwhile have another copper of liquor hot; and at two hours end begin to let off your first wort into the under-back. Receive a pailful of the first running, and throw it again upon the malt. You will find that the malt has sucked up half of your first copper of liquor; and therefore to make up your quantity of wort for your strong beer, you must gradually lade out of the second copper, and strew bowl after bowl over the malt, giving it time to soak through, and keeping it running by an easy stream, until you perceive you have about forty gallons, which in boiling and working will be reduced to thirty-six.

If you throw into the under-back (whilst you are letting off) about half a pound of hops, it will preserve it from foxing, or growing sour or ropy.

Your first wort being all run off, you must soften the tap of the mash tub; and take a copper of hot liquor for your second mashing, stirring up the malt as you did at first, and then cover

I LIKE MY KITCHEN
NEAT,
JUST LIKE MY
BOURBON.

it close for two hours more. Meanwhile you fill your copper with the first wort, and boil it with the remainder of the two pounds of hops, for an hour and a half, and then lade it off into the coolers.

Contrive to receive the hops in a sieve, basket, or thin woolen bag that is sweet and clean; then immediately fill your copper with cold liquor, renew your fire under it, and begin to let off your second wort, throw a handful of hops into the under-back, for the same reason as before: you will want to lade a few bowls full of liquor over the malt to make up the copper full of second wort; and when you have enough, fasten the tap and mash a third time after the same manner, and cover it close for another two hours; and then charge your copper with the second wort, boiling it for an hour with the same hops.

By this time you may shift your first wort out of the coolers into a working tub, to make room for the second wort to come into the coolers; and then your copper being empty, you may heat as much liquor as will serve you to lade over the malt, or, by this time, rather grains, to make up your third and last copper of wort, which must be bottled with the same hops over again; and then your coolers are discharged of your second wort, to make room for the third; and when they are both of a proper coolness, they may be put together before you set them a working.

During the time of shifting your liquors out of the copper, it is of consequence to take care to preserve it from receiving damage by burning: you should always contrive to have the fire low, or else to damp it at the time of emptying, and be very expeditious to put in fresh liquor.

OF WORKING THE LIQUOR

In this, regard must be had to the water: liquor naturally grows warm in working; therefore, in mild weather, it should be cold before it be set on, but a little warm in cold weather. The manner of doing it, is to put some good sweet yeast into a hand-bowl or piggin, with a little warm wort; then put the hand-bowl to swim upon the wort in the working tub, and in a little while it will work out, and leisurely mix with the wort, and when you find the yeast is gotten hold of the wort, you must look after it frequently; and if you perceive it begins to heat and ferment too fast, lade some of it out into another tub; and when grown cold, it may be put back again; or if you reserve some of the raw wort, you may check it leisurely, by stirring it in with a hand-bowl. The cooler you work your liquor, the better, provided it does but work well.

If you happen to check it too much, you may forward its working, by filling a gallon stone bottle with boiling water, cork it close and put the bottle into the working tub. An ounce or two of powdered ginger will have the same effect.

There are a variety of methods in managing liquors whilst they are working. Some people beat the yeast of strong beer and ale, once in two or three hours, for two or three days together. This they reckon makes the drink more heady, but withal

Part of the charm of a Four Roses Distillery tour is the story of how the facility got its name. I won't give it all away here, but suffice to say it involves a man, a woman and a proposal.

hardens it so as to be drinkable in two or three days; the last day of beating it in, (stirring the yeast and beer together) the yeast, as it rises, will thicken; and then they take off part of the yeast, and beat in the rest, which they repeat as often as it rises thick; and when it has done working, they turn it up, so as it may just work out of the barrel.

Others again do not beat it in at all, but let their strong drink work about two days, or until they see the ferment is over; and then they take off the top yeast, and either by a tap near the bottom, let it off sine, or else lade it out gently, to leave the sediment and yeast at the bottom.

This way is proper for liquor that is to be drank soon: but if it be to keep, it will want the sediment to feed upon, and may probably grow stale, unless you make artificial lees: This you may make of a quart of brandy, and as much flour of wheat as will make it into dough; put them in lumps into the bung hole as soon as it has done working. Or else take a pound of the powder of oyster shells and mix it with a pound of treacle or honey, and put it in soon after it has done working.

It would add to the goodness, as well as sining of your malt liquor, if you took two quarts of wheat, and make them very dry and crisp in an oven, or before the fire, and boil them in your first copper of wort. They would strain off with your hops, and might be put with them into the second copper.

OF THE FINING OF MALT LIQUORS

It is most desirable to have beer fine of itself, which it seldom fails to do in due time, if rightly brewed and worked; but as disappointments sometimes happen, it will be necessary to know what to do in such cases.

Ivory shavings boiled in your wort, or hartshorn shavings put into your cask just before you bung it down, will do much towards fining and keeping your liquor from growing stale.

Isinglass is the most common thing made use of in fining all sorts of liquors; they first beat it well with a hammer or mallet, and lay it in a pail, and then draw off about two gallons of the liquor to be fined upon it, and let it soak two or three days; and when it is soft enough to mix with the liquor, they take a whisk, and stir it about until it is all of a ferment, and white froth; and they frequently add the whites and shells of about a dozen of eggs, which they beat in with it, and put altogether into the cask; then with a clean mop-stick, or some such thing, stir the whole together; and then lay a cloth, or piece of paper over the bung-hole, until the ferment is over; and then bung it up close, in a few days it will fall fine. But if you want to fine only a small quantity, take half an ounce of unflacked lime, and put it into a pint of water, and stir it well together, and let it stand for two or three hours, or until the lime settle to the bottom; then pour the water off clear, and throw away the sediment; then take half an ounce of isinglass cut small, and boil it in the lime water until it dissolves; then let it cool, and pour it into the vessel, etc..

OF THE SEASON FOR BREWING

The season for brewing keeping-beer is certainly best before Christmas, for then your malt is in perfection, not having time to contract either a musty smell, dust or weavels, (an insect that eats out the heart of the malt) and the waters are then seldom mixed with snow; and then four pounds of hops will go as far as five in the spring of the year: For you must increase in the quantity of hops as you draw towards summer. But, in short, chuse moderate weather as much as you can for brewing, and if you have a kindly cellar besides to keep your liquor in, that will not be much affected by extremity of heat or cold, you may reasonably expect great satisfaction in your brewery. Avoid as much as possible brewing in hot weather; but if you are necessitated to brew, make no more than present drinking, for it will not keep.

TO MAKE ELDERBERRY-BEER OR EBULUM.

Take a hogshead of the first and strong wort, and boil in

the same one bushel of picked Elderberries, full ripe; strain off, and when cold, work the liquor in the hogshead, and not in an open tun or tub; and after it has lain in the cask about a year, bottle it; and it will be a good rich drink, which they call ebulum;

The barrel run and rick house at Willett Distillery in Bardstown. Slightly off the beaten path, the distillery's history dates back to shortly after the Civil War.

and has often been preferred to portwine, for its pleasant taste, and healthful quality.

N. B. There is no occasion for the use of sugar in this operation; because the wort has strength and sweetness enough in itself to answer that end; but there should be an infusion of hops added to the liquor, by way of preservation and relish. Some likewise hang a small bag of bruised spices in the vessel.

TO MAKE IMPROVED AND EXCELLENT WHOLESOME PURL

Take Roman wormwood two dozen, gentian-root six pounds; calamus aromatics (or the sweet flag root) two pounds; a pound or two of the galen gale-root; horse radish one bunch; orange peel dried, and juniper berries, each two pounds; seeds or kernels of Seville oranges cleaned and dried, two pounds.

These being cut and bruised, put them into a clean butt, and start your mild brown, or pale beer upon them, so as to fill up the vessel, about the beginning of November, and let it stand until the next season; and make it thus annually.

TO BREW STRONG BEER

To a barrel of beer take two bushels of wheat just cracked in the mill, and some of the flour sifted out of it; when your water is scalding hot, put it into your mash-vat, there let it stand until you can see your face in it; then put your malt upon that, and do not stir it; let it stand two hours and an half; then let it run into a tub that has two pounds of hops in it, and a handful of rosemary flowers; and when it is all run, put it into the copper, and boil it two hours; then strain it off, setting it a cooling very thin, and setting it a working very cool; clear it very well before you put it a working; put a little yeast to it; when the yeast begins to fall, put it into your vessel, put in a pint of whole grain, and

Photo courtesy of Buffalo Trace Distillery

The signature buffalo keeps watch over Warehouse C and the grounds of Buffalo Trace Distillery. The oldest continually operating distillery in the nation—and the only in Kentucky that was operational during prohibition—Buffalo Trace's history dates back to 1773 and includes such legends as E.H. Taylor, Jr., George T. Stagg, Albert B. Blanton, Orville Schupp, and Elmer T. Lee. Find out more at buffalotrace.com.

six eggs, then stop it; Let it stand a year, and then bottle it.

A good table-beer may be made, by mashing again, after the preceding is drawn off; then let it stand two hours, and let that run, and mash again, and stir it as before; be sure to cover your mashing-vat well; mix the first and second running together.

TO MAKE CHINA ALE

To six gallons of ale, take a quarter of a pound or more of China root, thin sliced, and a quarter of a pound of coriander seeds, bruised—hang these in a tiffany, or coarse linen bag, in the vessel, until it has done working; and let it stand fourteen days before you bottle.

TO MAKE ALE, OR ANY OTHER LIQUOR, THAT IS TOO NEW, OR SWEET, DRINK STALE.

To do this to the advantage of health, put to every quart of ale, or other liquor, 10 or 12 drops of the true spirit of salt, and let them be well mixed together, which they will soon do it by the subtle spirits penetrating into all parts, and have proper effect.

TO RECOVER SOUR ALE

Scrape fine chalk a pound, or as the quantity of liquor requires, more; put it into a thin bag into the ale.

TO RECOVER LIQUOR THAT IS TURNED BAD

If any liquor be pricked or fading, put to it a little syrup of clay, and let it ferment with a little barm, which will recover it; and when it is well settled, bottle it up, put in a clove or two, with a lump of loaf sugar.

DIRECTIONS FOR BOTTLING

You must have firm corks, boiled in wort, or grounds of beer; fill within an inch of the cork's reach, and beat it in with a mallet; then, with a small brass wire, bind the neck of the bottle, bring up the ends, and twist them over with a pair of pincers.

TO MAKE A QUARTER OF A HOGSHEAD OF ALE, AND A HOGSHEAD OF BEER, OF COOKED MALT

Take five strike of malt not ground too small; put in some boiling water, to cover the bottom of your mashing-vat before you put in your malt; mash it with more boiling water, putting in your malt at several times, that it may be sure to be all wet alike; cover it with a peck of wheat bran, then let it stand thus mashed four hours, then draw off three gallons of wort, and pour it upon that you have mashed, so let it stand half an hour more, until it runs clear, then draw of all that will run, and take two quarts of it to begin to work up with the barm, which must be about a pint and a half—put in the two quarts of wort at three times to the barm; you need not stir it until you begin to put in the boiled wort.

You will not have enough to fill your vessel at first; wherefore you must pour on more boiling water, immediately after the other has done running, until you have enough to fill a quarter of a hogshead, and then pour on water for a hogshead of beer.

As soon as the ale wort has run off, put a third part into the boiler—when it boils up, take off the scum, which you may put upon the grains for the small beer—when it is skimmed, put in a pound and an half of hops, having first sifted out the seeds, then put in all the wort, and let it boil two hours and an half, afterwards strain into two coolers, and let it stand to cool and settle, then put it to cool a little at a time, to the barm, and two quarts of wort, and beat it well together: every time you put the wort in, be sure you keep the settling out.

Suppose you brew early on Thursday morning, you may turn it at 9 or 10 on Saturday morning.

Do not fill your vessel quite full, but keep about three gallons to put in, when it has worked 24 hours, which will make it work again.

The Evan Williams Experience in Louisville, Kentucky. Features a five-story-high bourbon bottle façade (three dimensional on the first two floors) and indoor bourbon fountain. But leave your flask at home—that's not real bourbon in the fountain. For more information, visit evanwilliams.com.

As soon as it hath done working, stop it up, put the drink as cool as you can together; thus it will work well.

TO MAKE TREACLE BEER

Boil two quarts of water, put into it one pound of treacle or molasses, stir them together until they are well mixed; then put six or eight quarts of cold water to it, and about a tea cup full of yeast or barm, put it up in a clean cask or stein, cover it over with a coarse cloth, two or three times double, it will be fit to drink in two or three days.

Heaven Hill Bourbon Heritage Center in Bardstown greets guests with an impressive line-up of spirits. After-tour tastings are hosted in a giant tasting barrel. Heaven Hill was founded in 1935.

The second and third time of making, the bottom of the first beer will do instead of yeast.

If you make a large quantity, or intend it for keeping, you

must put in a handful of hops and another of malt, for it to feed on, and when done working, stop it up close.

The above is the best and cheapest way of making treacle beer, though some people add raisins, bran, wormwood, spices, such fruit, etc.. as are in season, but that is just as you fancy.

Indeed, many pleasant, cheap, and wholesome drinks may be made from fruits and the like if they are bruised and boiled in water, before the treacle is added.

The plan of manufacturing domestic wines, mead and small beer, once established and understood in a family, becomes easy—is considered a duty—and the females prepare as regularly for renewing them, as for baking, and doing every other branch of business. Many families amidst plenty of ingredients and means, rarely have a comfortable beverage under their roof—this is attributable to indolence, stupidity and want of knowledge. A little well timed, planning and system, with little more than usual labor, by the intelligent housewife, will cause comfort and plenty to reign throughout, and prove a fine and salutary example to society. Besides, the pleasure a lady derives from presenting a glass of good wine, in a nice clean glass to her welcome visitants, will always amply compensate for the trouble of manufacturing, and preparing it; but when the more intelligent pass a handsome and well merited compliment on the neatness and quality of her fare—she derives happiness from her industry, and a degree of pleasure approaching to exquisite. She may be esteemed one "who hath used her active faculties for the benefit of her family and society, and not only deserves well of society, but of heaven, for the judicious and liberal exercise of the mind, that god-like intellect, among the finest gifts of the munificent creator of worlds." But of her, who sitteth still and inactive, and doth not exercise those intellectual powers, it may be said "she is of an estrayed soul," and "hath buried her talent." And neither merits the attention of society, or the grateful love of her husband and family—and throws herself on the mercy of her God for forgiveness, for her numerous omissions, in withholding the exercise of her active faculties—presuming the being or individual, who is capable of the neglect of one duty, is capable of neglecting all—and though some little appearance may be kept up, yet conviction is eternally in the eye of the great judge—and not to be evaded.

Thus then the laws of society, morality and religion, requiring the active exercise of our person and faculties—offering the finest and most inducing rewards, the words of our language are capable of describing, in the health afforded from exercise; the example, from which society is benefitted; the pleasure derived from the approbation of our neighbors, and a conscientiousness of having performed our duties here, and living by the exercise of a proper system of economy, in a constant state of independence, always in possession of the means of alleviating the condition of the indigent and unfortunate in society—and relieving the wants of our friends—and above all, the hope of eternal happiness in the approbation of heaven hereafter.

If none can be obtained that is good, the following is a receipt to make it, viz.

Procure three wooden vessels of different sizes and apertures, one capable of holding two quarts, the other three or four, and the third five or six; boil a quarter of a peck of malt for about eight or ten minutes in three pints of water; and when a quart is poured off from the grains, let it stand in a cool place until not quite cold, but retaining that degree of heat which the brewers usually find to be proper when they begin to work their liquor. Then remove the vessel into some warm situation near a fire, where the thermometer stands between 70 and 80 degrees (Fahrenheit) and here let it remain until the fermentation begins, which will be plainly perceived within thirty hours; add then two quarts more of a like decoction of malt, when cool, as the first was; and mix the whole in the larger sized vessel, and stir it well in, which must be repeated in the usual way, as it rises in a common vat: then add a still greater quantity of the same decoction, to be worked in the largest vessel, which will produce yeast enough for a brewing of forty gallons.

FINIS

Kentucky Bourbon Tours
Courtesy of bourboncountry.com

BARDSTOWN and vicinity
- ➤ Barton's 1792 Distillery
- ➤ Heaven Hill Bourbon Heritage Center
- ➤ Limestone Branch Distillery
- ➤ Maker's Mark
- ➤ Willet Distillery

BOWLING GREEN
- ➤ Corsair Artisan Distillery

DANVILLE
- ➤ Wilderness Trail Distillery

FRANKFORT
- ➤ Buffalo Trace

LAWRENCEBURG
- ➤ Four Roses
- ➤ Wild Turkey

LEXINGTON and vicinity
- ➤ Alltech Lexington Brewing & Distilling Company
- ➤ Barrel House Distilling Company
- ➤ Hartfield & Co. Distillery
- ➤ Woodford Reserve

LOUISVILLE and vicinity
- ➤ Angel's Envy Distillery
- ➤ The Bulleit Experience at Stitzel-Weller
- ➤ Copper & Kings (Brandy aged in bourbon barrels)
- ➤ Evan Williams Bourbon Experience

- Grease Monkey Distillery at the Distilled Spirits Epicenter
- Jefferson's Reserve at Kentucky Artisan Distillery
- Jim Beam Urban Stillhouse
- Kentucky Peerless Distilling Co.
- Old Forester (opening fall 2017 on Whiskey Row)
- Michter's Micro-Distillery (opening 2018   on Whiskey Row)
- Rabbit Hole Distillery (opening fall 2017 in NuLu

NORTHERN KENTUCKY
- New Riff Distillery
- Old Pogue Distillery

PEMBROKE
- MB Roland Distillery

SHELBYVILLE
- Jeptha Creed

SHEPHERDSVILLE
- Four Roses Warehouses & Bottling Tours
- Jim Beam American Stillhouse

Note: This list will continue to be a work in progress. As readers will note, at least a couple of distilleries mentioned earlier in the book don't currently offer tours, but expect to do so in the near future. Be sure to check with bourboncountry.com, or visit the distillery's website for tour additions.

THOUGHTS FROM 1809, by Samuel McHarry

When I first entered on the business of Distilling, I was totally unacquainted with it. I was even so ignorant of the process, as not to know that fermentation was necessary, in producing spirits from grain. I had no idea that fire being put under a still, which, when hot enough, would raise a vapour; or that vapour when raised, could be condensed by a worm or tube passing through water into a liquid state. In short, my impressions were, that chop-rye mixed with water in a hogshead, and let stand for two or three days; and then put into a still, and fire being put under her, would produce the spirit by boiling up into the worm, and to pass through the water in order to cool it, and render it palatable for immediate use—and was certain the whole art and mystery could be learned in two or three weeks, or months at farthest, as I had frequently met with persons who professed a knowledge of the business, which they had acquired in two or three months, and though those men were esteemed distillers, and in possession of all the necessary art, in this very abstruse science; I soon found them to be ignorant blockheads, without natural genius, and often, without principle. Thus benighted, and with only the above light and knowledge, I entered into the dark, mysterious and abstruse science of distilling, a business professed to be perfectly understood by many, but in fact not sufficiently understood by any. For it presents a field for the learned, and man of science, for contemplation—that by a judicious and systematic appropriation and exercise of certain elements, valuable and salutary spirits and beverages may be produced in great perfection, and at a small expense, and little inconvenience, on almost every farm in our country. The professed chemist, and profound theorist may smile at my ideas, but should any one of them ever venture to soil a finger in the practical part of distilling, I venture to say, he would find more difficulty in producing good yeast, than in the process of creating oxygen or hydrogen gas. Scientific men generally look down on us, and that is principally owing to the circumstance of so many knaves, blockheads and conceited characters being engaged in the business. If then, the subject could be improved, I fancy our country would yield all the necessary liquors, and in a state of perfection, to gratify the opulent, and please the epicure. I had no difficulty in finding out a reputed great distiller, whose directions I followed in procuring every necessary ingredient and material for distilling, etc.. He was industrious and attentive, and produced tolerable yield, but I soon found the quantity of the runs to vary, and the yield scarcely two days alike. I enquired into the cause, of him, but his answers were, he could not tell; I also enquired of other distillers, and could procure no more satisfactory answer—some attributed it to the water, others to witchcraft, and etc. I found them all ignorant—I was equally so, and wandered in the dark; but having commenced the business, I determined to have light on the subject; I thought there must be books containing instructions, but to my surprise, after a diligent search of all the book-stores and catalogues in Pennsylvania, I found there was no American work extant, treating on this science—and those of foreign production, so at variance with our habits, customs, and mode of economy, that I was compelled to abandon all hope of scientific or systematic aid, and move on under the instructions of those distillers of our neighborhood, who were little better informed than myself, but who cheerfully informed me of their experiments, and the results, and freely communicated their opinions and obligingly gave me their receipts. In the course of my progress, I purchased many receipts, and hesitated not to procure information of all who appeared to possess it, and sometimes at a heavy expense, and duly noted down all such discoveries and communications—made my experiments from time to time, and in various seasons, carefully noting down the results. Having made the business my constant and only study, carefully attending to the important branch of making yeast, and studying the cause and progress of fermentation, proceeding with numerous experiments, and always studying to discover the cause of every failure, or change, or difference in the yield. I could, after four years attention, tell the cause of such change, whether in the water, yeast, fermentation, quality of the grain, chopping the grain, or in mashing, and carefully corrected it immediately. By a thus close and indefatigable attention, I brought it to a system, in my mind, and to a degree of perfection, that I am convinced nothing but a long series of practice could have effected. From my record of most improved experiments, I cheerfully gave receipts to those who applied, and after their adoption obtaining some celebrity, I found applications so numerous, as to be troublesome, and to be impossible for me to furnish the demands gratis, of consequence, I was compelled to furnish to some, and refuse others; a conduct so pregnant with partiality, and a degree of illiberality naturally gave rise to murmurs. My friends strongly recommended a publication of them, the plan requiring the exercise of talents, order and method, with which I presumed myself not sufficiently versed, I for some time obstinately refused, but at length and after reiterated solicitation, I consented to enter on the talk, under a flattering hope of affording useful information to those of my country engaged in the distillation of spirits from the growth of our native soil, which together with the following reasons, I offer as the only apology.**1st**. I observed many distillers making fortunes, whilst others exercising an equal share of industry, and of equal merit were sinking money, owing to a want of knowledge in the business. **2d**. In taverns I often observed foreign liquors drank in preference to those of domestic manufacture, though really of bad quality, possessing pernicious properties acquired from ingredients used by those in our commercial towns, who brew and compose brandies, spirits, and wines, often from materials most injurious to health, and this owing to so much bad liquor being made in our country, from which the reputation of domestic spirit has sunk. Whilst, in fact, we can make domestic spirits of various materials, which with a little management and age, will be superior to any of foreign produce. **3d**. By making gin, etc.. as good if not better, we might in a few years, meet those foreign merchants in their own markets, and undersell them; which we certainly could do, by making our liquors good, and giving them the same age. The transportation would of consequence improve them in an equal degree, for the only advantage their liquors of the same age have over our good liquors, is the mildness acquired by the friction in the warm hold of the ship in crossing the ocean. And moreover as liquors will be drank by people of all standings in society, I flattered myself I could improve our liquors, render them more wholesome to those whose unhappy habits compel a too free use of ardent spirits, and whose constitutions may have been doubly injured from the pernicious qualities of such as they were compelled to use. For there are in all societies and of both sexes, who will drink and use those beverages to excess, even when there exists a moral certainty, that they will sustain injury from such indulgence, and as an evidence of my hypothesis, I offer the free use of coffee, tea, etc.. so universally introduced at the tables of people of every grade. The wise Disposer of worlds, very happily for mankind, permits the exhibition of genius, mind and talents, from the peasant and lower order, as well as from the monarch, the lord, and the opulent. To Europe they of course are not confined—Genius has already figured in our hemisphere—The arts and sciences are becoming familiar, they rise spontaneously from our native soil, and bid fair to vie with, if not out-shine accomplished Europe. In possession, then, of all the necessary materials, ingredients and requisites, I would ask why we cannot afford ardent spirits and wines equal to those imported; and thus raise our character to a standing with other countries, and retain those millions of dollars at home, which are yearly shipped abroad for those foreign liquors, so common, so universally in use, and much of which so adulterated, as to be followed, when freely used, with unhappy consequences. Would men of capital and science, turn their attention to distillations, from the produce of our own country, preserve the liquor until age and management would render it equal, if not superior to any imported; is it not probable that it would become an article of export, and most sensibly benefit our country at large. Considerations such as those have combined to determine a publication of my work; fully apprised of the scoffs of pedants, kicks, bites and bruises of critics—but I hope they will find latitude for the exercise of a share of compassion, when I inform them candidly, that a mill and distillery, or still house, were substituted for, and the only college and academy in which I ever studied, and those studies were broken, and during the exercise of my business, as a miller and distiller. That it contains errors in the diction and perspicuity, I will readily confess—but that it is in substance true, and contains much useful information, I must declare as an indisputable fact. And though the road I travelled was a new one, without compass, chart, or even star to steer by, not even a book to assist me in thinking, or cheer me in my gloomy passage—seeking from those springs of nature, and inherent endowments for consolatory aid—pressing on a frequently exhausted mind, for resources and funds, to accomplish the objects of my pursuits—not denying but that I met many of my fellow-beings, who cheerfully aided me with all the information in their power, and to whom I now present my thanks—I must acknowledge, I think my labors and exertions will prove useful to those of less experience than mine, in which event I shall feel a more ample remuneration for my exertions, than the price asked for one of those volumes.

Could I have witnessed the publication of a similar work by a man of science and education, mine should never have appeared. But it would seem the learned and scientific have never considered a work of the kind as meriting their attention; a circumstance deeply to be regretted, as a finer coloring to a work of the same properties and value often procures celebrity, demand and currency. My object is to be useful, my style plain, and only labored to be rendered easy to be understood, and convey the necessary instruction to those who may honor this work with a perusal, or resort to it for information, and that it may be useful to my countrymen, is the sincere wish of—

The Author
The Practical Distiller

ORIGINAL 1809 INTRODUCTION

It is not more than twenty years since whiskey was first offered for sale in the seaport towns in large quantities; and then, owing to its badness, at a very low price. Since that period it has been gaining ground yearly, and at this time, it is the second great article of commerce, in the states of Pennsylvania and Maryland.

In the interior of these states, it has nearly excluded the use of foreign distilled spirits, and I fancy might be made so perfectly pure and nice, as to ultimately supersede the use of any other throughout the United States.

To assist in effecting this, the greatest attention should be paid to cleanliness, which in a distillery is absolutely necessary, the want of which admits of no excuse, where water is had without price.

If a distiller does not by a most industrious well-timed care and attention, preserve every utensil perfectly sweet and clean, he may expect, notwithstanding he has well attended to the other branches, but indifferent whiskey and not much of it.

If, for instance, every article, or only one article in the composition of yeast be sour or dirty, that one article will most assuredly injure the whole; which being put into a hogshead of mashed grain, soon imparts its acidity or filth to the whole mass, and of course will reduce the quantity and quality of the spirit yielded from that hogshead. Cleanliness in every matter and thing, in and about a distillery becomes an indispensable requisite, without a strict observance of which the undertaker will find the establishment unproductive and injurious to his interest. Purity cannot exist without cleanliness. Cleanliness in the human system will destroy an obstinate itch, of consequence, it is the active handmaid of health and comfort, and without which, decency does not exist.

Care is another important and necessary consideration, and a basis necessary, on which to erect a distillery, in order to ensure it productive of wealth and reputation. Care and industry will ensure cleanliness; an eye of care must be extended to everything, that nothing be lost, that everything be in its proper place and order, that everything be done in due time; the business must be well timed, and time well economised, as it ranks in this, as in every other business very high. Let a judicious attention be paid to care, cleanliness, and industry, and when united with a competent knowledge of the different branches of the distilling business, the character of a complete practical distiller is perfect.

With such a distiller, and a complete still-house, furnished with every necessary utensil for carrying on the business—it cannot fail to prove a very productive establishment, and present to the world, from the materials of our own farms, a spirit as wholesome, and well flavored and as healthy as any spirit whatever—the produce or yield of any country, provided it be permitted to acquire the same age.

What a grand and great idea strikes the thinking scientific mind, on entering a complete and clean distillery, with an intelligent cleanly distiller, performing his duty in it.

To see the four elements, each combining to produce (with the assistance of man) an article of commerce and luxury, and at the same time, a necessary beverage to man. The earth producing the grain, hops and utensils, which a combination of fire and water reduces into a liquid by fermentation, and when placed in the still to see air engaging fire to assist her in reducing the liquid that fire and water had produced, into a vapor, or air, and afterwards to see fire abandoning air, and assisting water to reduce it into a liquid by means of the condensing tubes, and then to consider the number of hands employed in keeping the distillery a going, will present one other patriotic idea. The farmer with all his domestics and people, engaged in the cultivation of the rye, corn, etc.. The wood choppers—the hauling—the coopers engaged in making casks—the hands engaged in feeding cattle and the pork—hauling, barreling and selling the whiskey, spirits, pork, etc.. The produce of the distillery, presenting subject for commerce, and employ for the merchant, mechanic and mariner—and all from our own farms.

After seeing the distillery afford employment for so many hands, bread to their families, and yielding the means of an extensive revenue and increase of commerce—with a flattering prospect of completely annihilating the use of foreign liquors in our country, and thereby saving the expenditure of millions of dollars; and ultimately rendering our liquors an article of export and source of wealth—I presume every mind will be struck with the propriety of encouraging a branch of business so promising in wealth and comfort.

The receipts are intended to convey all the instruction necessary in the science of distilling, and producing from the growth of our own farms, the best spirits of every description, and such as I flatter myself will supersede the use of all imported liquors, and thereby fulfil the views and wishes of—

The Author
The Practical Distiller

One Final Note:

Seriously. This really is the end of the book. I hope you had as much fun reading this as I had creating it.

I'm so grateful to all who've helped bring this together and supported me along the way—you know who you are—and I fear that in trying to name each of you I would forget someone. From hanging out at your distilleries, to layout discussions over coffee at Panera and countless texts and emails, you all shined as I knew you would.

For those of you who'd like to chat more, let's meet up on Instagram: @militarywriter. You can also email me at: beth@talkbourbon.com or beth@bethwrightunderwood.com. For now, pull out your favorite drinking glass. I think it's time we all enjoy a little Kentucky Bourbon. ☺